Early Child Development in China

Early Child Development in China

Breaking the Cycle of Poverty and Improving Future Competitiveness

Kin Bing Wu
Mary Eming Young
Jianhua Cai

THE WORLD BANK
Washington, D.C.

ISBN (paper): 978-0-8213-9564-6
ISBN (electronic): 978-0-8213-9565-3
DOI: 10.1596/978-0-8213-9564-6

Cover photo: provided by NPFPC; *Cover design:* Debra Naylor of Naylor Design

Library of Congress Cataloging-in-Publication Data has been applied for.
Wu, Kin Bing, 1951–
Early child development in China : breaking the cycle of poverty and improving future competitiveness/ by Kin Bing Wu, Mary Eming Young, and Jianhua Cai.
    p. cm.
  Includes bibliographical references.
  ISBN 978-0-8213-9564-6—ISBN 978-0-8213-9565-3 (electronic)
1. Children—China—Social conditions. 2. Children—Services for—China. 3. Child development—China. 4. Child welfare—China. 5. Poverty—China. I. Young, Mary E., 1955- II. Cai, Jianhua. III. World Bank. IV. Title.
  HQ792.C5W83 2012
  305.2310951—dc23   2012022756

Contents

Boxes

Figures

Tables

Foreword

Since the implementation of economic reform in 1978, real GDP per capita (in 2000 U.S. dollars) in China has grown more than 12-fold, from about $165 in 1978 to $2,206 in 2009, lifting hundreds of millions out of poverty. China has become the second largest economy in the world. This is a miracle in itself.

Yet, in the course of its rapid economic growth, income disparity has widened. In 2009, 35.97 million people still lived in absolute poverty, with a per capita annual income of less than RMB1,196 ($176). Children under 12 years of age accounted for 18 percent of this extremely poor group. If the benefits of China's prosperity are to reach all of its citizens, more than economic growth will be needed to reduce absolute poverty and inequality. Investments in health, nutrition, and education, and the extension of these services to the poor, will be needed to sustain broad-based development, improve social cohesion, and advance from a middle-income economy to a high-income one.

Since China has already universalized nine years of compulsory education and has rapidly expanded enrollment in post-compulsory education, the biggest challenge for its human development strategy is in early child development (ECD) for children from the prenatal stage through the first six years of life. Investments in ECD are among the most cost-effective strategies to break the intergenerational transmission of poverty, improve productivity, and sustain competitiveness in the long run.

Neuroscientists have found that the most effective interventions for active brain development take place from birth through two years of age. International evidence shows that investments in ECD yield high economic returns because early learning is far more productive than later, remedial interventions, and because they are more cost-effective relative to other interventions. For example, ECD programs in the United States yield rates of return in the order of 7–18 percent. ECD attendees in Columbia were 100 percent more likely to be enrolled in higher grades, and their counterparts in Bangladesh performed 58 percent better on standardized tests. PISA test scores for 15-year-old students who attended at least one year of preprimary school were significantly higher across the developing and developed worlds.

In spite of these benefits, the poor's inability to pay for services has resulted in the underutilization of services, and the long time horizon of recouping ECD investments has resulted in the underprovision of such services. This argues for an increased public role in the funding of ECD. Lessons from around the world suggest that China can break the cycle of poverty and enhance its future growth by targeting assistance to poor women through prenatal care and nutrition, and to children from ages 0–6 through health interventions, nutrition, parenting education, early learning, and preprimary education.

The publication of this report is timely and can contribute to addressing China's inequality, which is a major objective of China's 12th Five-Year Plan. *Early Child Development in China: Breaking the Cycle of Poverty and Improving Future Competitiveness* is the first World Bank report of its kind for China, and it provides relevant lessons for other countries that are contemplating investments in ECD to address inequality and to sustain growth.

Justin Yifu Lin
Senior Vice President and Chief Economist
World Bank

Foreword

In the past 30 years, China has reached the target of lifting 500 million people out of poverty. The rate of increase in human development indicators has become the second fastest in the world, allowing China to enter the ranks of middle-income countries. As the most populous country, accounting for one-fifth of the world's population, its transformation has been unprecedented in human history.

Scientific evidence and international experience in the past 10 years have found that early child development (ECD) is key to human development, as it lays the foundation for the rest of life. Early child development includes physical, psychological, emotional, language, behavioral, and social development. Experience in the early years of life will determine healthy development and happiness in the rest of life.

Through a comprehensive collaboration with the World Bank, we have developed this book on ECD through a review of the literature and administrative data, and analysis of data from a household survey to assess the policy options for promoting ECD.

Currently, about 16 million babies are born every year in China, and about 50 million children in China are between the ages of 0–3. Research has found that investment in ECD is the most cost effective strategy to improve human development. In China's demographic transition, the population of children and youth is declining in absolute numbers, and the investment of raising them can increase on a per capita basis. As such, ECD provides many advantages. Although China has made important progress in ECD, it still faces important challenges as public investments to date have been inadequate and coverage is limited. Children in rural and remote areas have limited access to the opportunity for development and education. ECD has not been part of the public finance and social security system.

Promoting ECD is key to improving the quality of China's population, and to advance from a populous country to a country of strong human resources. It is the first step to China's sustainable economic growth and development. We hope that this book, *Early Child Development in China: Breaking the Cycle of Poverty and Improving Future Competitiveness*, will promote collaboration between various organizations, agencies, and ministries within China and internationally.

The National Population and Family Planning Commission will coordinate with relevant departments on policy and resources, and mobilize a network of local cadres and public services to systemically, comprehensively, and scientifically promote the physiological, psychological, behavioral, and social development of young children. The goals are to alleviate poverty and promote family development and to increase investment and services in rural areas to benefit society and more healthy families.

Dr. Beige Zhao
Vice Minister
National Population and
Family Planning Commission

Preface

This study has been in the making since 2009. It was prepared during a time when China was charting its course of development under the 12th Five-Year Plan (2011–2015). The study began with an agreement between the World Bank and China's National Population and Family Planning Commission (NPFPC) for a collaborative study on early child development (ECD). Concurrently, China's Ministry of Education invited the World Bank to conduct an overall review of the education sector, in order to provide it with inputs and suggestions as it prepared China's *National Plan for Medium- and Long-Term Education Reform and Development (2010–2020)*. In reviewing achievements and challenges in the education sector, the Bank found that there was much room for expanding and improving preprimary education for children ages 3–6. The Ministry of Education appreciated the Bank's identification of this need and set ambitious goals for preprimary education in the *National Education Plan*.

The collaborative study with NPFPC on ECD went into greater depth. It extended coverage to children ages 0–3, and it included health and nutrition. The result was a comprehensive study on ECD in China. Many key messages of the book were incorporated into the World Bank's invited inputs to China's 12th Five-Year Plan (2011–2015) and the upcoming publication, *China 2030*, a collaborative work by the World Bank and the Development Research Center of the State Council.

The initial report of this study was disseminated in Beijing on February 22, 2011, at a seminar cohosted by the World Bank and NPFPC. Officials from the State Council, the National Development and Reform Commission, the Ministry of Finance, the Ministry of Health, the Ministry of Education, the All-China Federation of Women, delegates from the National People's Congress, and representatives from 12 provincial governments, as well as representatives of universities, international organizations, and embassies, attended the seminar, which was chaired by Vice Minister Dr. Beige Zhao of the NPFPC. A consensus emerged about the importance of public investment in ECD, particularly the need to expand services for the poor and disadvantaged. The Chinese version of the report was published in China by the Population Press in June 2011.

Since the promulgation of the 12th Five-Year Plan, which has a strong focus on improving people's livelihood, the government of China has issued a series of guidelines—on the development of women and children, on poverty reduction and the development of rural areas, on health system reform, and on services to the elderly. These guidelines amplified and reinforced its position regarding targets, measures, responsibility for implementation, and monitoring and evaluation arrangements. Piloting interventions in health and education for children ages 0–6 have also been initiated since the 12th Five-Year Plan was announced. These policies and measures will have a lasting impact on human development in China and will play a key role in China's transformation from a middle-income to a high-income country. To reflect these new policies, the report was revised and updated.

Acknowledgments

This study is the result of a collaboration between the World Bank and the National Population and Family Planning Commission (NPFPC) of China. The study was designed and prepared by Dr. Kin Bing Wu (lead education specialist, World Bank), with major intellectual inputs from Dr. Mary Eming Young (senior adviser, Harvard University) and Mr. Jianhua Cai (director-general, NPFPC). The study benefited from the contribution of Prof. Albert Park of Chinese University of Science and Technology (sampling of the household survey in Hunan Province and the questionnaire on household finance); Prof. Nianli Zhou of East China Normal University (measurement of social and cognitive development of three-year-olds in the Hunan survey); Prof. Xinzheng Shi of Tsinghua University (multivariate analysis of the Hunan household survey); Ms. Yunbo Liu of the Chinese University of Hong Kong (finance of early childhood development and education); and Mr. Prateek Tandon of the World Bank (editorial inputs). The study also drew on the commissioned work of Dr. Yaohua Dai of the Capital Institute of Pediatrics in Beijing (child health and safety) and Prof. Yan Liu of Beijing Normal University (adaptation and piloting of Early Development Index). Ms. Sabrina Terry and Ms. Tao Su provided program support.

The authors are grateful to the World Bank management of the East Asia and Pacific Region—particularly Dr. Luis Benveniste, Dr. Emmanuel

Y. Jimenez, Mr. Klaus Rohland, Dr. Eduardo Velez, and Dr. Xiaoqing Yu—for their support.

The authors are grateful to Dr. Beige Zhao, vice minister of NPFPC, for the overall support of the study, and to Ms. Meilan Gu, Ms. Yanping Luo, and Mr. Jifang Tan of the Hunan Provincial Population and Family Planning Department (HPFPD) for collaborating on the household survey. One hundred and twenty specialized cadres in Hunan were mobilized to assist in the survey. Staff from the Training and Communication Center of NPFPC—Ms. Sisi Guo, Ms. Snow Jiang, Ms. Freda Lian, Ms. Summer Liu, Ms. Rui Sun, Ms. Marcia Wu, Ms. Xinyu Xu, Ms. Audrey Hu Yun, and Ms. Wendy Zhao—verified data, translated the report into Chinese, and facilitated the dissemination of the report.

Graduate students from East China Normal University—Xiaoxia Chen, Huan Li, Jing Wang, Yu Wang, Yu Wang, Fangfang Xu, Ping Zhou, and Benqin Zuo—assisted in the fieldwork and data entry of the Hunan survey. Volunteers from the Hunan Wan Ying kindergarten—Jiao Chen, Yao Chen, Chao Chen, Ying Li, Xu Lin, He Li, Heng Liu, Wenqian Liu, Yang Liu, Shiqi Wang, Dongdong Wen, Huiyu Xiao, Jun Yang, Xiaoya Yu, and Juan Zhong, Jing Zhong, and Linghui Zhou—supported the direct observation and testing of the sampled children. Save the Children's China Program provided financial support for the Hunan survey.

The report was reviewed within the World Bank by Dr. Christoph Kurowski (sector leader), Dr. Sophie Naudeau (human development specialist), Dr. Yidan Wang (senior education specialist), and by a panel of external reviewers convened by the NPFPC. Dr. Shuquan Wang of the Central Educational Science Research Institute and Dr. Yi Zheng of Capital Medical University reviewed the issue paper and instruments. Dr. Donald Bundy (lead specialist, school health), Dr. Chaoying Liu (senior evaluation specialist), Dr. Liping Xiao (senior education specialist), and Dr. Xiaoyan Liang (senior education specialist) of the World Bank provided helpful advice. Dr. Hana Brixi (then chief of Social Policy and Economic Analysis, UNICEF); Dr. Yunying Chen (senior research fellow, China National Institute of Education Science); and Mr. John Giszczak (director of finance, Save the Children China Program) provided insightful comments.

Contributors

Jianhua Cai (蔡建华) is the director-general of the Training and Communication Center at in the National Population and Family Planning Commission of China (NPFPC), where he is responsible for training programs and the early childhood development programs. Before joining the NPFPC, he headed the Planning Division of the Science and Technology Commission of the Shanghai municipal government, where he worked for almost 12 years. He has extensive experience in policy making, regulation formation, and program planning and development. A biologist by training, he holds an MBA from the China-Europe International Business School.

Yunbo Liu (刘云波) is a Ph.D. candidate in economics of education in the Chinese University of Hong Kong. She studied economics in Peking University and did research in the China Institute for Educational Finance Research (CIEFR) of Peking University.

Albert Park is a chaired professor of social science, a professor of economics, and a senior research fellow at the Institute for Advanced Study at the Hong Kong University of Science and Technology. He also is a research fellow at the Institute for the Study of Labor (IZA), in Bonn, Germany, and the Centre for Economic Policy Research, in London. His research focuses on education and health, labor, aging, and poverty in China. He holds a Ph.D. in economics from Stanford University.

Xinzheng Shi (施新政) is an assistant professor of economics at the School of Economics and Management at Tsinghua University, China. He holds a Ph.D. in economics from the University of Michigan.

Kin Bing Wu (邬健冰) is lead education specialist in the East Asia and the Pacific Region of the World Bank. During more than 20 years at the Bank, she has worked in 26 countries in East Asia, South Asia, and Latin America. She has covered low-income and middle-income economies, transitional economies, and post-conflict countries. Her World Bank and academic publications have dealt with the finance and efficiency of education systems and public policies toward education. She has focused particularly on achieving equity in education for rural populations and disadvantaged communities. Before joining the Bank, she taught at the Chinese University of Hong Kong and Hong Kong Polytechnic University. She holds an Ed.D. in economics of education from Harvard University.

Mary Eming Young (杨一鸣) is a senior adviser to Harvard University's Center on the Developing Child. A pediatrician and public health specialist, she is a globally recognized expert on child health and development and maternal and child health systems. In 30 years at the World Bank, she guided efforts in global health and child health and development. She received her M.D. from the University of Wisconsin and her Ph.D. in public health from Johns Hopkins University.

Nianli Zhou (周念丽) is an associate professor in the department of early childhood education and director of the Psychological Research Laboratory at the East China Normal University. She holds a Ph.D. from the East China Normal University.

Executive Summary

Since the implementation of economic reform in 1978, real GDP per capita in China (in constant 2000 U.S. dollars) has grown more than 12-fold, from about $165 in 1980 to $2,206 in 2010, lifting hundreds of millions out of poverty. However, the rural-urban income gap remains wide: The average annual income per capita in rural areas (RMB5,153, or $758 in current prices) was less than one-third that in urban areas (RMB17,175 or $2,526) in 2009. Some 36 million people still lived in absolute poverty, with per capita annual income of less than RMB1,196 ($176) (NBS 2009)—less than the World Bank's poverty line of $1.25 a day. Children under age 12 accounted for 18 percent of this group. In November 2011, China revised its poverty line upward, to RMB 2,300 ($366) (Xinhua News 2011), roughly equivalent to $1 a day. As a result, the number of people living under the poverty line was adjusted upward to 128 million, or slightly less than 10 percent of the population.

There is a growing realization in policy circles that economic growth alone cannot reduce absolute poverty and inequality, that investments in human development and improved access to service are needed to sustain growth and improve social cohesion. China has already universalized nine years of compulsory education and rapidly expanded enrollment in postcompulsory education. The biggest gap in its human development strategy is in early child development (ECD): care, development, and education for children from birth to six years of age. Investments in ECD are one of the most cost-effective strategies for breaking the intergenerational transmission of poverty and improving productivity and social cohesion in the long run. Furthermore, due to China's rapidly aging population, the burden of sustaining growth and supporting the elderly will fall on the young children of today.

Neuroscience and longitudinal studies of ECD find that both positive and negative experiences in early life beginning at conception influence the development of the brain and biological systems for life. Nutrition, care, nurturing, and negative experiences beginning during gestation (pollutants, neurotoxins, infection, and the mother's health, well-being, and stress level) influence how genes are expressed and the architecture and function of the brain. Lack of access to nutrition and health care, neglect, and nonenrollment in ECD programs are associated with lower educational attainment and achievement, which, in turn, reduce lifetime earnings and contribute potentially to disruptive social behavior.

The results of the Organisation for Economic Co-operation and Development's (OECD) 2009 round of the Programme for International Student Assessment (PISA)—a cross-national comparison of mathematics, science, and reading skills of 15-year-olds—provide evidence of the effect of ECD on subsequent academic achievement. Shanghai had the highest scores among 74 participating countries and territories. There was a difference of more than 60 points (about 10 percent of the difference in the scores in Shanghai) between 15-year-olds who had attended preprimary school for more than a year and those who had not. This evidence suggests that China can further boost its overall student achievement by universalizing ECD services.

Nobel laureate James Heckman and his coauthor (Carneiro and Heckman 2003) show that investing in ECD yields the highest economic returns; healthy early development is far more productive than later, remedial interventions. The internal rates of return of rigorously evaluated programs range from 7 percent to 18 percent—higher than the average rates of return to financial capital.

Although China has made enormous progress in maternal and child health and has universalized nine years of compulsory education, the challenge in bridging the gap in ECD between rural and urban areas remains enormous. About 16 million babies are born every year in China, 61 percent of them in rural areas. In 2008, 34 percent of 6-month-olds in rural areas had anemia, and 14.9 percent of rural

3-year-olds were stunted; in poor rural counties, stunting was as high as 21 percent. The rural and urban gap in height and weight widens with age. According to Ministry of Health data from 2005 (MOH 2009), on average, at age 6 urban boys weighed 1.7 kilos more than rural boys, and urban girls were 2.4 kilos heavier than rural girls. Urban boys were 2.6 centimeters taller than rural boys on average, and urban girls were 2.4 centimeters taller than rural girls. Rural children were also more likely to be deficient in micronutrients.

In 2011, under-5 mortality in China was 16 per 1,000 live births, far below developing countries' average of 72. Yet the rural-urban gap remained large: under-5 mortality in rural areas was 19 per 1,000 live births, 2.7 times higher than the 7 per 1,000 in urban areas. Between 1991 and 2011, maternal mortality fell from 80 to 26 per 100,000 live births, and the rural-urban gap narrowed. The maternal mortality rate is still far higher than in Japan (6 per 100,000 live births) or the United Kingdom (12 per 100,000 live births), however.

Variations across provinces are dramatic. Nationwide, 90 percent of pregnant women receive prenatal check-ups, with the figures ranging from 67 percent in Tibet to 99 percent in Beijing. The share of newborns weighing less than 2,500 grams ranges from 0.08 percent in Shanghai and 0.28 percent in Beijing to 4.2 percent in Jiangxi and Yunnan and 6.5 percent in Tibet.

An estimated one-third of rural children are left behind by parents who have migrated to work. They are usually cared for by their grand-mothers, who tend to have lower educational attainment and less knowl-edge than their parents about nutrition, health, and education.

Although the national gross enrollment ratio in kindergarten increased from 21 percent in 1985 to 51 percent in 2009, only about one-third of rural children have access to preprimary education. In 2008, about 48 percent of these children attended only a single year of preschool (not 2 to 3 years of kindergarten). The emotional, social, and cognitive development of the left-behind children has increasingly dis-played signs of stress.

Goals of, Responsibility for, and Financing of Early Child Development Services

China has long believed that the future of the country lies with its chil-dren. The following guidelines and plans point to a strengthened policy on ECD.

- The *National Guidelines on Family Education* (2010) reflects a heightened emphasis on family education as a foundation for nation building.
- *China's National Plan Outline for Medium- and Long-Term Education Reform and Development (2010–2020)* (henceforth the *Educational Plan*) set targets for expansion of preprimary education for the next decade (State Council 2010a) (see annex table 5A.2).[1]
- The *Guidelines on the Development of Preprimary Education* (State Council 2010b) provide concrete suggestions about how to expand preprimary education, including instructing various levels of governments to coordinate planning, ensure the age-appropriateness of kindergarten curriculum, and integrate expenditures into the budget to ensure that the mandate is funded (see annex table 5A.3).
- *The 12th Five-Year Plan (2011–2015)* (NPC and CPPCC 2011), which provided the guiding principles and specific direction in all sectors for a five year period, reaffirmed the principles of improving people's livelihood and social integration in its social and economic policies.
- The *Guidelines on Chinese Women Development (2011–2020), the Guidelines on Chinese Children Development (2011–2020), the Guidelines on Poverty Reduction and Development of Chinese Rural Areas (2011–2020), and the Plan for Population Development in the 12th Five-Year Plan* (State Council 2011b, 2011c, 2011d) propose goals and targets; multisectoral interventions that cover health, education, social protection, and law; assign responsibilities to government agencies; integrate expenditures into the regular budget to ensure the mandate is funded; and identify indicators and evaluation criteria in the development in these areas. These call for tighter intersectoral coordination. The multipronged approach within and across these sectors reinforces the principles of gender equality, protection of children's rights, development of children ages 0–6, and support for disadvantaged children (including those who are left behind in rural areas, orphans, children with special needs, poor children, rural children, and children of ethnic minorities) (see annex tables 5A.4–5A.6).

Various entities are responsible for promoting ECD. The National People's Congress legislates to protect the rights of women and children and regulates services for them. The State Council promulgates policies and directives concerning women and children. The National Working Committee on Women and Children under the State Council is the highest body safeguarding the rights of women and children and coordinating affairs across government departments and nongovernmental organizations. Although cooperation among ministries has been increasing, the overall policy, coordination, administration, finance, and service delivery of ECD remains somewhat diffused. Implementing the well-intended far-sighted policy is a challenge.

Policy and supervision are the responsibilities of line ministries, whereas service provision and financing are the responsibilities of county governments in rural areas and district governments in municipalities. The key policy makers and service providers are as follows:

- Services to children under age 3 are provided mainly by the health sector. The Ministry of Health sets policy, organizes maternal and child health services, and monitors outcomes. It promulgates regulations on health and hygiene in nurseries and kindergartens and guides and monitors related work. The services provided by the health departments in local governments include prenatal and postnatal care, free vaccination, and free annual check-ups for children (laboratory tests are not free).
- The Ministry of Human Resources and Labor Security defines occupational standards for people caring for children ages 0–3, provides in-service training, and certifies caregivers.
- The National Population and Family Planning Commission is responsible for raising the capability of the population. Its mandate extends from family planning to young children's development from birth to age 3. It has established about 50 demonstration centers that provide services for maternal and child medical care and early stimulation (see box 3.1 in this book for details).
- The Ministry of Education sets policy for and oversees the implementation of preprimary education for children ages 3–6, sets curricular standards, drafts laws and regulations, and monitors and evaluates preprimary education. Education departments at the provincial, municipal, county, and district levels operate and finance public kindergartens, approve and oversee private kindergartens, set the level of fees charged by public and private kindergartens, provide preservice and in-service teacher education, collect statistics, and inspect kindergartens.
- The Ministry of Civil Affairs considers ECD an integral part of community services. It has overall responsibilities for family welfare, child protection, and disaster relief. Local governments finance and operate orphanages for abandoned children and orphans.

- The All-China Women's Federation is the leading advocate of the rights of women and children. Through family education and development, it promotes the protection of these rights.
- The private sector, including nonprofit and for-profit organizations, operates about 68 percent of nurseries and kindergartens in China.

Poor and rural children, particularly ethnic minorities, have lower access to preprimary education than other children. Although the majority of China's children live in rural areas, about 57 percent of enrollment in preprimary education is in cities and towns. Rural children are underserved because county governments' weak fiscal capacity limits supply and parents' inability to pay for services dampens demand.

The expansion of coverage for preprimary education in the last two decades was driven largely by growth in cities, which masked the decline in service provision to rural areas. The number of rural kindergartens fell by half, from 130,030 in 1986 to 71,588 in 2010. In contrast, the number of kindergartens rose from 24,500 to 35,845 in cities and from 18,700 to 42,987 in county towns. Enrollment followed a similar pattern.

Disparities in quality have exacerbated the rural/urban inequality in access. In 2010, the student-to-teacher ratio was 9:1 in cities, 16:1 in county towns, and 28:1 in rural areas. Qualified teachers were also unevenly distributed across cities, towns, and rural areas.

The disparity in access to service is partly the result of inadequate public expenditure. In 2009, enrollment in preprimary education in the public sector accounted for 7 percent of total enrollment in the public education system, but budgetary spending on it was only 1 percent of the total public budgetary expenditure on education.

China's budgetary spending on preprimary education was about 0.1 percent of GDP in 2008—much lower than the OECD average public spending on preprimary education of 0.4 percent of GDP (OECD 2011). Iceland was the highest-spending country in 2008, devoting 1.0 percent of its GDP to preprimary education; Israel and Spain spent about 0.8 percent; and Denmark, Sweden, Hungary, Mexico, France, the Russian Federation, and Chile each spent 0.6–0.7 percent.

Preprimary education is financed mostly on a cost-recovery basis, irrespective of whether it is public or private. About 68 percent of kindergartens are private, enrolling about 47 percent of students. Monthly fees range from RMB130 ($19) to RMB3,000 ($441). The low end covers mostly food and learning materials. The more expensive kindergartens also provide air conditioning and Chinese-English bilingual education. In addition to these fees, most kindergartens charge "sponsorship fees," which can range from RMB3,000 to RMB12,000 a year ($441–$1,765). Sponsorship fees are used to purchase equipment (HDTV, computers, DVDs, musical instruments) and to pay for repairs and maintenance, security, and decoration of the premises.

To put these fee levels in perspective, in 2008 the average rural income was RMB5,153 ($758). Without policy intervention to ensure equity, ECD could become education for the elite.

Determinants of Child Development Outcomes and Policy Implications

To inform policy about potential areas of intervention, in March 2010 the Training and Communication Center of the National Population and Family Planning Commission and the World Bank jointly conducted a household survey in Hunan Province. The survey addressed the following questions:

- How large are the disparities in child development outcomes between rural and urban areas, boys and girls, Han and ethnic minorities, and children cared for by their parents and children left behind?
- Do enrollment in kindergarten, access to health check-ups, and good child-rearing (parenting) practices make a difference in child development outcomes, after controlling for rural and urban resident status, ethnicity, gender, left-behind status, educational attainment of mother and other caregivers, and family income?

Hunan was chosen because its economy is based largely on agriculture, its per capita GDP is at the lower-middle-income level, it is a major labor-exporting province, and it has several ethnic minority groups. The survey took a sample of 15 counties/districts in cities and an additional sample of 2 minority autonomous counties for comparison with the main sample. A questionnaire administered to the primary caregiver collected information on household characteristics, access to services, and child-rearing practices. The survey also included direct observation and testing of the cognitive skills of 3-year-olds. The survey collected data from 1,011 rural and urban households and their 3-year-old children.

The findings confirm the inequity evident from the macro data. About 32 percent of children in the 15 counties in the main sample, and 48 percent of children in the 2 minority counties, were left behind by their migrant parents and cared for by their grandparents or others. Urban children, Han children, children cared for by their mother, and children who attended kindergartens were heavier and taller and had better cognitive scores (though not necessarily better social development scores) than rural children, ethnic minorities, left-behind children, and children who did not attend kindergarten. Although girls were shorter and lighter than boys, they tended to have higher social and cognitive scores in the 15 counties. Minority girls living in the two minority counties had the lowest weight and height of all groups.

A multivariate analysis of the data in the 15 counties of the main sample used weight, height, social development, and cognitive development as outcome measures. The analysis began by regressing demographic characteristics on the aforementioned child development outcomes. It then added four sets of independent policy variables to see whether they made any difference. The policy variables were attendance in kindergarten and parent-child classes; access to medical checkup and immunization; child-rearing practices (such as frequency of reading to the child, playing with the child, discipline, and watching TV); and dietary habits.

The findings are as follows:

- Different factors affected weight, height, social development, and cognitive development.
- Adding the policy variables—nutrition, health checkups, good child-rearing practices, enrollment in day care or kindergarten, and providing caregivers with access to information—reduced the negative effects of household income and mother's education on weight, height, social development, and cognitive development.
- Weight at birth remained a consistent predictor of weight and height at age 3, suggesting the importance of prenatal care and nutrition. Ethnic minorities were taller than Han children after holding other variables constant, suggesting that proper nutrition and health interventions are important.

These findings have two important policy implications. First, because birth weight is a consistent predictor of subsequent physical growth, interventions at the prenatal stage can help ensure the healthy development of children. Second, interventions that provide or subsidize nutrition, health care, and parenting education; provide information and training to caregivers; and increase attendance in kindergarten can improve children's weight, height, and social and cognitive development, particularly among the poor.

The Way Forward

The social benefits and high economic returns to society suggest that universalization of nutrition, health, and education to all children under the age of 6 should be a long-term goal. Given resource and capacity constraints, however, the 12th Five-Year Plan period (2011–15) could adopt (1) a two-pronged pro-poor approach that includes targeted interventions to the extremely poor through the government's antipoverty program, and (2) expansion of ECD as a mainstream social service, with fiscal transfers to the Western and Central regions.

Including Early Child Development in the Government's Antipoverty Program

The prime target of intervention should be the estimated 3.3–4.0 million children under age 6 among China's 36 million people in absolute poverty, whose average annual income is less than RMB1,196 ($176) per capita. Geographic targeting is possible because 66 percent of these extremely poor people live in the Western region, 25 percent in the Central region, 5 percent in the Eastern region, and 3 percent in the Northeastern region. Ethnic minorities will likely benefit disproportionately from these interventions, because China's preferential family planning policy allows them to have more children, and yet a large proportion of them is poor.

In 2008, about 45 percent of poverty reduction funds were spent on improving the means of production, and 32 percent went toward improving infrastructure; only 1.8 percent was allocated to social services, including education and training. The *Guidelines for Poverty Alleviation and Rural Development (2011–20)* specifically cites ECD services as an intervention for extremely poor children and sets enrollment targets for them (80 percent enrollment in kindergarten three years before entering grade 1 by 2015 and basic universalization of pre-primary education by 2020).

The government has distinguished ECD services for two age groups. This book recommends these goals for interventions for the 0–3 age group:

- improve prenatal care, nutrition, and information for extremely poor pregnant women and ensure free hospital delivery, in order to increase the probability of delivering a healthy baby;
- improve the nutritional and health status of young children by providing a nutritional package (that includes micronutrients) for children 6- to 36-months-old, in order to overcome the nutritional deficiency after weaning from breastfeeding;
- improve the knowledge of mothers and primary caregivers about health, nutrition, child care, and nurturing (or positive stimulation), in order to foster emotional, social, and cognitive development;
- foster the formation of networks of caregivers in local communities to share experiences and create opportunities for children to interact with their peers, in order to develop language and social skills. International experience shows that home-based or community-based approaches that facilitate interaction and training of mothers and caregivers by people knowledgeable about nutrition, health, and nurturing can be highly cost-effective.

Interventions for the 3–6 age group are primarily center-based, and focus on the improvement of school readiness skills, which include language, numeracy, and psychosocial skills, through the provision of preprimary education. International experience shows that most children could realize cognitive and noncognitive gains by participating in learning activities 15–30 hours a week (3–6 hours a day) nine months a year. Parenting education could be used to deliver curriculum-based information for caregivers to implement at home, to be complemented by peer interaction.

Making Early Child Development Part of an Expanded Mainstream Service

ECD interventions that are successful in reducing income and social gaps between poor and nonpoor populations are multisectoral in nature, including health, nutrition, education, water, hygiene, sanitation, and legal protection. To make ECD a mainstream service, there is a need to set up a policy framework to provide the vision and targets, so that different policy areas that affect young children can be linked and coordinated across multiple line ministries and their local counterparts toward a common set of outcomes.

The 12th Five-Year Plan has heralded a turning point for ECD in China, as the series of guidelines on women and children's development, poverty reduction and rural development are cross-sectoral in their scope of interventions, with clearly spelled out targets and implementation responsibility within a monitoring framework.

China's demographic composition—the relatively small share of young children, the low child dependency ratio, and increasing urbanization—is highly favorable for investment in ECD. The share of the population ages 0–14 declined from 41 percent in 1964 to 19 percent in 2008, making it more feasible and affordable to provide high-quality care, development, and education to all children. The mainstreaming of ECD as a regular social service could eventually lead to universal coverage for the 0–6 age group.

By improving the quality of human development, ECD improves future citizens' productivity and competitiveness, thereby enabling China to overcome the challenges of an aging population and the transition into a high-income economy.

Note

1. The targets are as follows: gross enrollment ratio (GER) for children starting kindergarten three years before grade 1 to increase from 51 percent in 2009 to 60 percent in 2015, GER for children starting kindergarten two years before grade 1 to increase from 65 percent to 70 percent, and GER for children entering kindergarten one year before grade 1 to increase from 74 percent to 85 percent (see annex table 5A.2 for the targets). The GER targets for 2020 are 70 percent for children starting kindergarten three years before grade 1, 80 percent for children starting kindergarten two years before grade 1, and 95 percent for children starting kindergarten one year before grade 1 (see annex table 5A.2).

References

All-China Women's Federation, the National Population and Family Planning Commission, the Ministry of Education, the Ministry of Civil Affairs, the Ministry of Health, the Civilization Office of the Central Communist Party Committee, and the China National Committee for the Well-being of Youth. 2010. *National Guidelines on Family Education.* Beijing. (中华全国妇女联合

会、国家人口和计划生育委员会、教育部、民政部、卫生部、中央文明办、中国关心下一代工作委员会。全国家庭教育指导大纲).

Carneiro, P., and J. Heckman. 2003. "Human Capital Policy." NBER Working Paper 9495, National Bureau of Economic Research Cambridge, MA. www.nber.org/papers/w9495.

MOH (Ministry of Health). 2009. *China Health Statistics Yearbook*. Beijing: China Xiehe Medical University Press.

NBS (National Bureau of Statistics of China). 2009. *Poverty Monitoring of Rural China*. Beijing: China Statistics Press.

OECD (Organisation for Economic Co-operation and Development). 2011. *Education at a Glance: OECD Indicators*. Paris: OECD.

State Council. 2010. *China's National Plan Outline for Medium- and Long-Term Education Reform and Development 2010–2020*. Beijing: State Council. http://www.gov.cn/jizg/2010-07/29. (国务院。国家中长期教育改革和发展规划纲要).

———. 2011. *Guidelines on Poverty Reduction and Development of Chinese Rural Areas (2011–2020)*. Beijing: State Council. http://www.gov.cn/jrzg/2011-12/01. (国务院。中国农村扶贫开发纲要).

Xinhua News. 2011. "China Raises Poverty Line by 80 pct to Benefit over 100 mln." (news.xinhuanet.com/english2010/china/2011-11/29).

Abbreviations

ACFW	All-China Federation of Women
BRIC	Brazil, Russia, India, and China
ECD	Early Child Development
CCTV	China Central Television Station
CDC	China Center for Disease Prevention and Control
CPPCC	Chinese People's Political Consultative Conference
FYP	Five-Year Plan
GDP	Gross domestic product
GER	Gross enrollment ratio
MOCA	Ministry of Civil Affairs
MOE	Ministry of Education
MOH	Ministry of Health
MOF	Ministry of Finance
MHRSS	Ministry of Human Resources and Social Security
NBS	National Bureau of Statistics
NDRC	National Development and Reform Commission
NER	Net enrollment ratio
NPC	National People's Congress
NPFPC	National Population and Family Planning Commission

NWCCW	National Working Committee for Women and Children
OECD	Organisation for Economic Co-operation and Development
PISA	Programme for International Student Assessment
RMB	Renminbi (Chinese national currency)
UNICEF	United Nation Children's Fund
UNDP	United National Development Programme
WHO	World Health Organization

Currency equivalents: US$1.00 = RMB6.8 (2010)

CHAPTER 1

The Importance of Early Child Development

Since the implementation of economic reform in 1978, real gross domestic product (GDP) per capita (in constant 2000 U.S. dollars) in China has grown more than 12-fold, from about $165 in 1980 to $2,206 in 2009, lifting hundreds of million people out of poverty (World Bank database).[1] China's progress in human development has been equally impressive. Average life expectancy at birth increased from 57.0 years in 1957 to 73.5 years in 2009, thanks to improved food security, immunization, and health care (China Daily 2011a; NPC and CPPCC 2011).[2] Illiteracy was reduced from 80 percent in 1949 to 4 percent for men and 10 percent for women in 2009 (see annex table 1A.1).

Sustained efforts in education have fundamentally changed the country's human resource endowment. Between 1985 and 2009, the net enrollment ratio (NER) in primary education rose from 96.0 percent to 99.5 percent—no small achievement, as reaching the remaining hardest-to-reach children is costly and challenging.[3] Over the same period, the gross enrollment ratio (GER) increased from 20 percent to 51 percent in preprimary education, from 52 percent to 99 percent in junior-secondary education, from 29 percent to 79 percent in senior-secondary education (including technical and vocational training education [[TVET]), and from less than 3 percent to 24 percent higher education (MOE various years).[4] China's educational indicators compare favorably with those of other countries (see annex table 1A.1). Its investments in education have sustained its economic growth, which, in turn, provides more resources for further expansion and deepening of human capital, forming a virtuous cycle (World Bank 2009a, 2009b, 2010a).

This remarkable progress notwithstanding, China faces formidable challenges in its goal of becoming a high-income economy. Among the challenges, three affect human development in particular. First, income inequality has been growing, as reflected in the increase in the Gini coefficient, a statistical measure of inequality, from 0.29 in 1981 to 0.47 in 2010 (World Bank database; China Daily 2010).[5] The gap between rural and urban areas is widening. In 2009, average annual per capita income in urban areas (RMB17,175, or $2,526) was 3.3 times that of rural income (RMB5,153, or $758), and about 36 million people lived in absolute poverty, with a per capita annual income of less than RMB 1,196 ($176)—less than the World Bank's poverty line of $1.25 a day. Children under age 12 accounted for 18 percent of this group (NBS 2009a).

In November 2011, China revised its poverty line upward, to RMB 2,300 ($366) (Xinhua News 2011), roughly equivalent to $1 a day.[6] As a result, the number of people living under poverty was adjusted upward to 128 million, or slightly less than 10 percent of the population.[7] Although the raising of the poverty line shows an implicit commitment to use government programs and resources to reduce poverty, the magnitude of the challenge is enormous.

Second, China has experienced massive rural to urban migration, with an estimated 211 million rural residents migrating to cities in 2009, and the average age was 27.8 (NPFPC 2010). Because of the high cost of living in urban areas—and China's household registration system, which affixes legal residency (hukou) and the rights to social services, land use, and social protection based on a person's family origin in rural or urban areas—many migrants leave their young children in rural areas, to be cared for by grandparents or other relatives. An estimated 55 million children of compulsory school age were left behind by their parents in 2005 (interview with Mr. N. Yang, Deputy Director-General of Department of Basic Education I, Ministry of Education, June 2010). Children who migrate to urban areas with their parents often find it difficult to access social services. Many attend fee-charging private schools, often of poorer quality than public schools (Wang and Wu 2008). Although policy in recent years requires that receiving localities provide social services to migrant children, implementation is not uniform. Ironically, China's successful economic development is undermining the foundation of the family. But reforming the household registration system, which is being considered and piloted, will take time, as reform would affect other institutions, including pensions, insurance, land use, housing, and urban planning.

Third, China's population is aging, just as the country is trying to make the transition from a middle-income to a high-income economy. The proportion of people age 60 and over was 13.3 percent in 2011 and is projected to double by 2030 (State Council 2011a). The burden of increased productivity and competitiveness to sustain economic growth and support the older population will fall on people who are young children today.

China has to race against time to implement policies in the medium term to address these problems. Sustaining its economic growth and attaining a higher standard of living for all require transformation from past and present reliance on capital- and labor-intensive production to production driven by knowledge and innovation. Investing in human development, particularly early child development, lies on the critical path to achieving China's goals.

Worldwide, poverty and inequality begin in pregnancy and continue after birth. Children born into poor families have a higher probability of having lower birth weight because of poor nutrition. Low-income parents are more likely to have low levels of education attainment and less knowledge of good child-rearing practices. They have to work instead of spending more time with their children to stimulate their development. They are also less likely to have access to public services, such as water, sanitation, health, and education. A recent study finds that inequality of opportunity accounts for 20–50 percent of observed economic inequality in Latin America (Ferreira and Gignoux 2007).

Investments in early child development (ECD) are one of the most cost-effective strategies for breaking the intergenerational transmission of poverty and improving equality of opportunity. Evidence from neuroscience and longitudinal studies indicates that experiences during the first six years of life affect the development of the brain and, consequently, the cognitive and socioemotional development of children in subsequent stages of their lives.

Recognizing the urgency to further reduce poverty and address rising inequality, in recent years the government of China has issued a series of farsighted policies, which are presented in chapter 2 in this book.

This chapter examines the indicators of child development in China to identify accomplishments and understand the scope of the challenges. It draws on the conceptual framework of child development in annex figure 1A.1 for organizing the indicators and discussion. It then reviews evidence on how ECD can change the trajectory of life chances, improve the capabilities of the population, and yield high economic returns to society. Box 1.1 provides the definition of terms used in this book.

Box 1.1

Institutions that Care for and Educate Children in China before They Enter Primary School

Three main types of institutions care for and educate children under the age of 6 in China:

- *Nurseries* are equivalent to crèches or day care centers in other countries for children age 3 and younger, except that some Chinese nurseries have boarding facilities for working parents. Nurseries focus predominantly on custodial care. Care providers are not supervised by education authorities but by other government authorities, depending on their affiliation.

- *Kindergartens* are of two to three years' duration before primary school. They focus on the development of social skills, hygienic habits, and literacy and numeracy for children ages 3–6. The Ministry of Education uses the term *kindergarten* to include "independent kindergartens, kindergartens attached to primary schools, and independent preschool classes." In this book, the term is used inclusively to cover all institutions that provide development and education to children before they enter grade 1.

- *Preschool classes* refer to the single year of education before children enter grade 1. Structurally, it is equivalent to the last year of kindergarten, in which children are prepared for literacy and numeracy. The one year of education before grade 1 serves the same function as kindergarten in the United States. However, in the United States, kindergarten is an integral part of public education. In China, unlike grades 1–9, preschool classes are neither compulsory nor free. In rural areas, the early childhood education experienced by most children

(continued next page)

Box 1.1 *(continued)*

before they enter grade 1 is one year of preschool classes, not two to three years of kindergarten.

• *Preprimary education* is used by the Organisation for Economic Co-operation and Development (OECD) to refer to education for children age 3 and older before they enter grade 1. It is roughly equivalent to the term *kindergarten* in China. This book uses the term *preprimary education* in the same way that OECD does when referring to this subsector.

• *Early child development* (ECD) refers explicitly to a child's early development. ECD is used in this report rather than the nonspecific *early childhood development*. ECD comprises the care, development, and education of children from birth to age 6.

Box Table 1.1.1   Types of Early Child Development Institutions in China

Term	Duration	Age	Focus
Nurseries	Up to 3 years	Up to 3 years old	Care
Kindergarten	2–3 years	2–5 or 3–6 years old	Development and education, with focus on literacy and numeracy in the last year
Preschool	1 year before grade 1	5 or 6 years old	Preparation for literacy and numeracy
Preprimary education	1–3 years	3 years old and older	OECD term for subsector of education before grade 1

Source: Authors.

Status of China's Children

The number of children in China under the age of 6 declined in the last two decades, falling from 161 million in 1990 to about 100 million in 2008 (NBS 2009a). Children under age 6 account for about 7.5 percent of China's 1.3 billion citizens (figure 1.1), less than the 11 percent in the Organisation for Economic Co-operation and Development countries (OECD 2008). China's policy of family planning allows both the government and households to allocate more resources to improving maternal and child health.

The under-5 mortality rate in developing countries declined by about 28 percent between 1990 and 2008, falling from 100 deaths per 1,000

Figure 1.1   Age Structure of China's Population

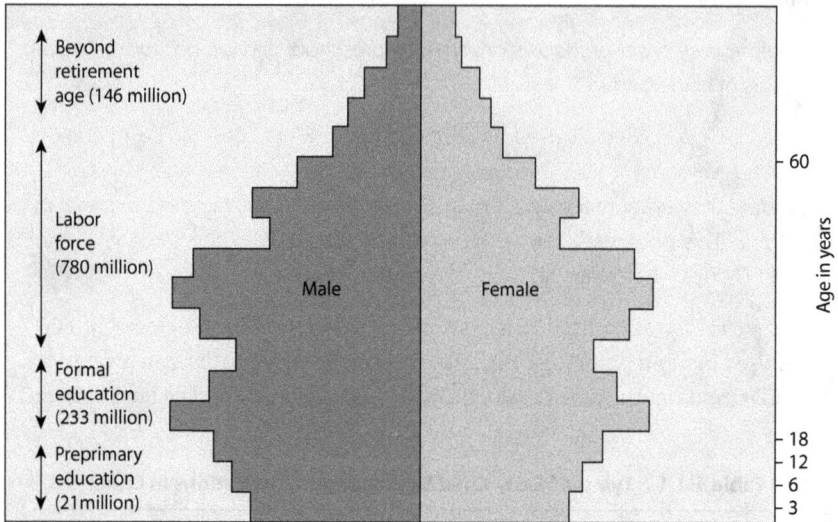

Sources: Author, based on data from U. S. Census Bureau 2010; World Bank 2009a.
Note: Total population in 2010 was 1.338 billion.

live births to 72 (UN).[8] Between 1991 and 2011, the under-5 mortality in China declined from 61 deaths to 16 deaths per 1,000 live births (figure 1.2), much faster than the developing world's average. A rural-urban gap remains, however. In 2011, the under-5 mortality in urban China was 7 per 1,000, close to the rate in developed countries. In contrast, the rate in rural China was 19 per 1,000, about the same as the 2008 national average in Brazil (19 per 1,000) and higher than the Russian Federation (12 per 1,000) (figure 1.3).

Maternal mortality in China also declined, falling from 80 deaths per 100,000 live births to 26 between 1991 and 2011 (see figure 1.2). Although China still has some way to go to reach the rate in developed countries, it fares better than other BRIC (Brazil, Russian Federation, India, and China) countries (see figure 1.3). The rate of decline in maternal mortality in rural China was faster than that in urban China. The relatively small difference in maternal mortality in urban (25 deaths per 100,000 live births) and rural (27 deaths per 100,000 live births) areas indicates that China has found an effective way to address disparity and improve social development (figure 1.4). Compared with Japan and the United Kingdom, however, there is still room for improvement.

Figure 1.2   Maternal and Under-5 Mortality in China, 1991 and 2011

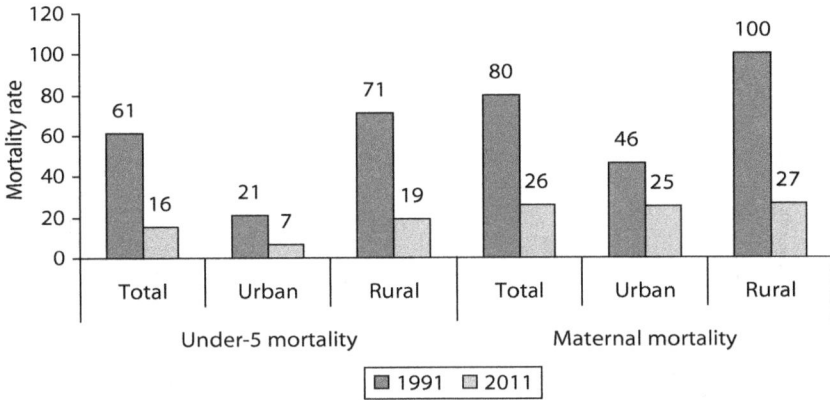

Source: Authors, based on data in MOH 2011.
Note: Under-5 mortality rate is deaths per 1,000 live births. Maternal mortality rate is deaths per 100,000 live births.

Figure 1.3   Under-5 Mortality in Selected Countries, 2010

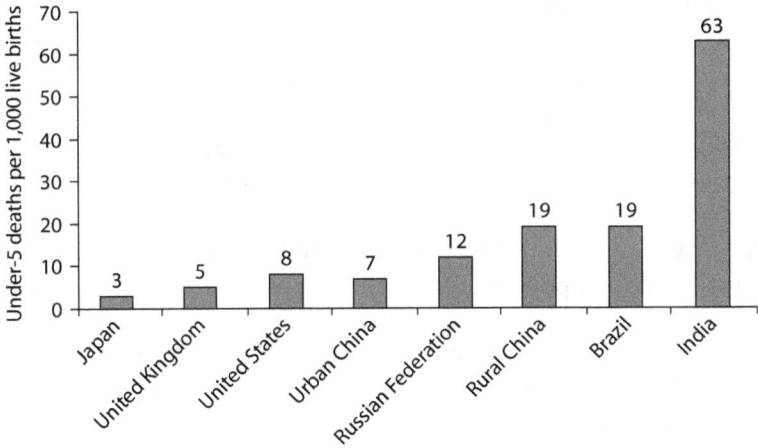

Source: UN Interagency Group 2011.

The average birth weight of babies in China is 3,228 grams, comparable to the level of developed countries, according to the World Health Organization's Growth Standards. The proportion of babies born with a birth weight below 2,500 grams decreased from 3.7 percent

Figure 1.4   Maternal Mortality in Selected Countries, 2008

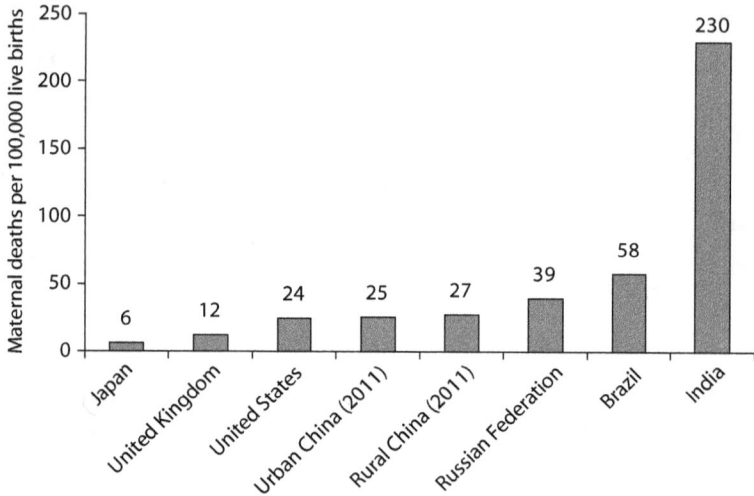

Source: WHO 2011.

to 2.4 percent between 1991 and 2008. These figures are much lower than the average for middle-income countries of 15 percent. The proportion of severely malnourished children also declined, falling from 3.1 percent in 2000 to 1.9 percent in 2008. These figures compare very favorably with the average for middle-income countries of 13 percent, and immunization reached 99 percent of children in 2008 (MOH 2009).

Improvements in nutrition and health are attributable to the success of China's national poverty alleviation program since 1993 and to policies that resulted in a 7 percent average annual increase in the per capita income of farmers (NBS 2009c). Exemption from the agricultural tax, direct subsidies for agriculture, establishment of the grain cropping risk management fund, free compulsory education, expansion of health services in rural areas, and medical insurance contributed to improved nutrition and health.

The challenge to improving child health and development remains enormous, however. About 16 million babies are born in China every year, 61 percent of them in rural areas.[9] Variations across provinces are large. The national rate of prenatal checkup is 90 percent, ranging from 67 percent in Tibet to 99 percent in Beijing (MOH 2009). The proportion of children under 5 with severe malnutrition ranges from 0.28 percent in Beijing and 0.08 percent in Shanghai to 4.2 percent in Jiangxi and Yunnan and 6.5 percent in Tibet (figure 1.5).

Prematurity, inevitably associated with low birth weight, is a leading cause of under-5 mortality in China. The percentage of underweight babies at birth has declined over time, but the percentage of underweight children is higher at age 5 than at birth because of undernutrition in early childhood. Poor rural counties have higher percentages of underweight-for-age children than rural areas in general: in 2008, 7.3 percent of 2-year-olds in poor rural counties were underweight, compared with 5.0 percent in all rural areas (figure 1.6). The situation is the same for stunting (low height-for-age): 21 percent of 2-year-olds in poor rural counties were stunted, compared with 16 percent in all rural areas (figure 1.7). Stunting at age 2 is associated with lower cognitive development later in life (Chen 2009).

Figure 1.5   Percentage of Children Under Age 5 in China with Severe Malnutrition, by Province, 2008

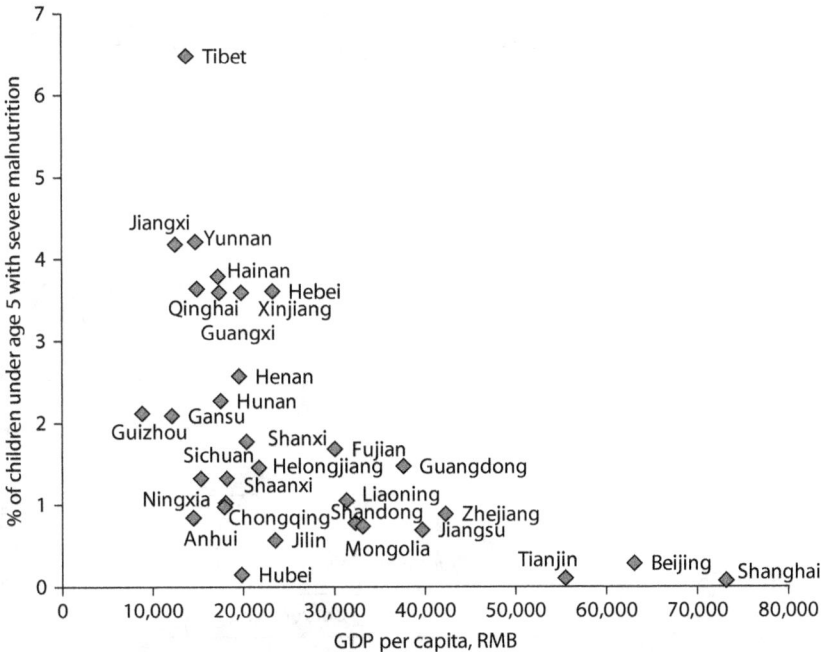

Figure 1.6   Percentage of Underweight Children in Rural China, by Age, 2008

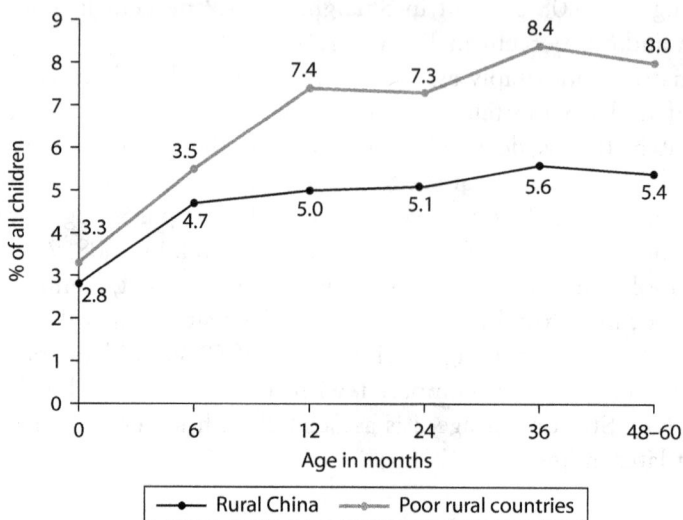

Source: Chen 2009.
Note: Underweight at birth is defined as weighing less than 2,500 gram.

Figure 1.7   Percentage of Stunted Children in Rural China, by Age, 2008

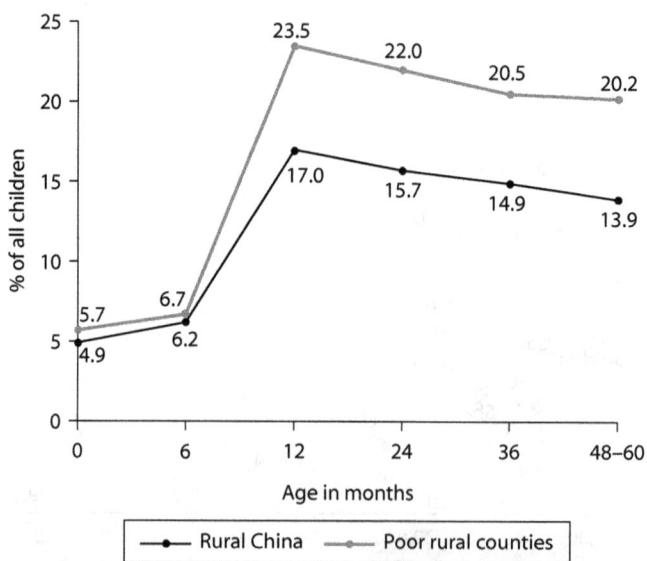

Source: Chen 2009.
Note: Stunting is defined as height for age that is more than two standard deviations below the median of the reference population.

The rural-urban disparity in height and weight increases with age. In 2005, at age 6, urban boys on average weighed 1.72 kilos more than rural boys, and urban girls were 2.44 kilos heavier than rural girls (table 1.1). In height, the rural-urban difference was about 2.6 centimeters for boys and 2.4 centimeters for girls.

Rural children, particularly children living in remote areas, are more likely to be deficient in iron, calcium, and zinc, especially after the recommended period of six months of exclusive breastfeeding. Supplemental nutrients are not generally available in their diet.

Figure 1.8 presents the rural-urban differences in anemia prevalence of children under age 5. Despite improvement, the rural anemia prevalence at age 6 months in 2008 was 34 percent, still higher than the 30 percent in urban areas in 2005.

Investing in early child nutrition is a highly efficient way to improve the health, cognitive ability, and productivity of the population. For every 1 percent of low height-for-age, physical productivity in adulthood is reduced by 1.4 percent. Nutritional intervention for children under age 3 could result in an 8 percent increase in annual wages for one z-score difference in weight-for-age at age 3 (Chen 2009).

Today, Chinese parents have higher educational attainment than their parents. But another trend is undercutting the potential benefits of higher parental education: the practice in which rural parents migrate to urban areas for work, leaving their children behind in the care of grandparents or other relatives. These caregivers generally have lower educational attainment than the parents and are less knowledgeable about nutrition, health, and good child-rearing practices. There are still traditional child-rearing practices that overlook the critical importance of adult child interaction and proper nutrition (box 1.2). Some rural grandparents, for example, believe the advertisement that instant noodles are nutritious and sell their farm-raised eggs to buy instant noodles for their grandchildren. In doing so, they unintentionally contribute to the under-nutrition of their grandchildren.

There is no reliable figure on how many children under age 6 have been "left behind" by their parents in rural areas. In the survey of Hunan Province commissioned for this study in 2010, about a third of 3-year-olds in the main sample were left behind. There is likely to be large variation by locality. In schools located in major labor-exporting counties in Sichuan, for example, 80 percent of children in primary and secondary schools do not have both parents living with them, according to the World Bank review mission of the China Basic Education in Western

Table 1.1   Physical Development of Chinese Children at Birth, Age 3, and Age 6, 2005

	Boys		Girls		Boys		Girls	
Setting/age	Weight (kg)	Standard deviation	Weight (kg)	Standard deviation	Height (cm)	Standard deviation	Height (cm)	Standard deviation
Rural at birth	3.32	0.40	3.19	0.39	50.4	1.7	49.8	1.7
Urban at birth	3.33	0.39	3.24	0.39	50.4	1.2	49.7	1.7
Rural at age 3	14.05	1.65	14.22	1.66	97.2	3.9	96.2	3.9
Urban at age 3	15.13	1.75	14.8	1.69	98.9	3.8	97.6	3.8
Rural at age 6	20.79	2.89	20.11	2.87	117.4	5.0	116.5	5.0
Urban at age 6	22.51	3.21	22.55	2.94	120	4.8	118.9	4.6

Source: MOH 2009.

Figure 1.8   Prevalence of Anemia in Children under Age 5 in Rural and Urban China, 2005 and 2008

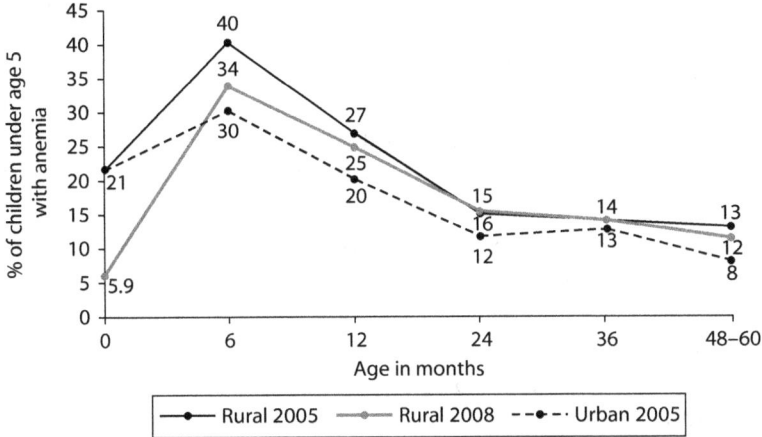

Source: Chen 2009.
Note: Urban data were available only for 2005.

Box 1.2

Depriving Children of Stimulation by "Sandbag Rearing"

Some traditional views on child development in China are contrary to the science-based evidence. For example, children under the age of 6 were traditionally considered to be passive and in a state of "not understanding." A traditional method of rearing young children, commonly practiced in parts of Shandong and Hubei provinces even as recently as the 1990s, was known as "sandbag rearing." A newborn was laid in a bag of fine sand, which acted as a diaper and was changed once a day. The baby was visited only when being fed by the mother. After a period of no stimulation, children raised this way became quiet, ceasing to express emotions. Babies were generally left in the bag for one to two years.

Comparison of randomly selected "sandbag children" ages 7–16 who were deprived of stimulation for more than a year when they were babies with a similar group raised more normally found that the average IQ of sandbag children was one standard deviation below that of children in the control group. Children left in the sandbag for 24 months scored 1.5 standard deviations below children left in the sandbag for 12–18 months (Xie and Young 1999).

Areas Project of 2009. Schools have been relied on to assume the role of guardians of these children. These trends highlight the important role of ECD services in providing care and guidance in children's physical, moral, social, and cognitive development, compensating for the lack of parental involvement.

Another demographic trend also poses a challenge to child development. China has a significant sex imbalance at birth. In the 1960s and 1970s, the sex ratio at birth was 103–107 boys for every 100 girls. This ratio rose to 119.5 in 2009, before declining slightly to 118 in 2010 (China Daily 2011b). Skewed sex ratios may lead to social problems in the future. The government has adopted a series of policies and actions to improve the survival of girls, increase women's status, and promote gender equality. Changing social attitudes and practices will take time, however.

Although the GER in preprimary education in China increased from 21 percent in 1985 to 51 percent in 2009, coverage is still low in comparison with some countries at the level of development China aspires to reach. For example, the GER in preprimary education in Mexico is 106 (figure 1.9).

Moreover, there is a mismatch between the distribution of the population ages 0–6 and the number of students in kindergartens. In 2008, about 61 percent of China's population ages 0–6 lived in rural areas, but enrollment in rural kindergartens accounted for just 43 percent of the total (figure 1.10). Underenrollment in rural areas reflects both supply constraints (caused by county governments' weak fiscal capacity to provide services) and demand constraints (caused by parents' inability to pay for such services). These issues are discussed in chapters 2 and 3 in this book.

Poor children are less likely to be healthy or to have access to ECD services. Insufficient investments in their development and education are likely to affect their lifetime earnings and potential contribution to society, undermining China's social cohesion and competitiveness. The next section reviews the evidence on the effects of early interventions on human development to assess the potential opportunity cost of neglecting ECD.

Evidence on the Importance of Early Child Development

The healthy development of children depends on a reciprocal and dynamic interaction between nature and nurture. Whereas genes determine when brain circuits are formed, experience shapes the connections

Figure 1.9   Enrollment in Child Care for Children under Age 3 and in Preprimary Education for Children Ages 3–5, Selected Countries, 2008

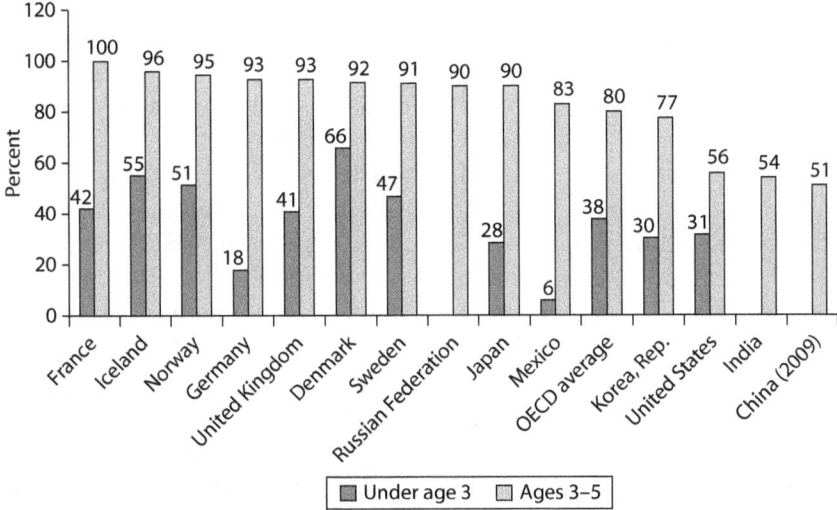

Sources: OECD family database; World Bank database; and State Council 2010.

Figure 1.10   Distribution of Children Ages 0–6 and Number of Students in Kindergartens in Rural and Urban China, 2008

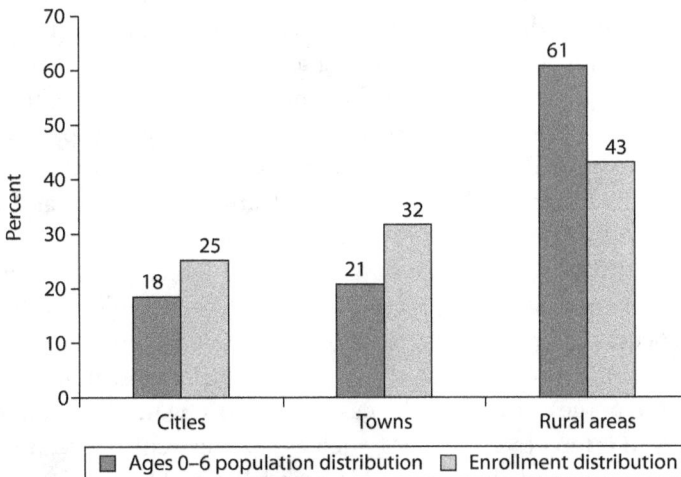

Sources: NBS 2009c; MOE 2009.

among the billions of neurons and the function of neurons. Experiences comprise social interactions (for example, between parents and children); physical exposures (for example, toxins); and material resources (for example, nutrition).

Adult-child interaction is crucial in the very early years of life. It has a major effect on neural function and brain development. Sensory stimulation from the environment—starting from the intrauterine environment (which is affected by nutrition, pollutants, drugs, infections, and the mother's health and stress level) through the early years after birth—influences how genes are expressed (turned "on" or "off") and the architecture and function of the child's brain. Both positive and negative experiences—such as poverty, malnutrition, abuse, and neglect—affect brain development (Alderman 2011). Evidence from longitudinal studies, such as the Adverse Childhood Experiences Study, the Bucharest Early Intervention Project, and the Dunedin Longitudinal Study, show that adversity in utero and during early life can increase risks for adult diseases (including obesity, type 2 diabetes, high blood pressure, and heart disease) and behavior problems (including addiction, aggression, and depression) (Keating 2011; McCain, Mustard, and McCuaig 2011).

Brain development is continuous, with each developmental step influencing the next one (Ellis, Jackson, and Boyce 2006). The brain's architecture and a child's developing abilities build from the bottom up in a hierarchical sequence. Simple circuits and skills develop first, setting the foundation for the building of more advanced circuits and skills. The sequence of brain development relating to experience—that is, the stimulation of sensing pathways (seeing, hearing, touching, smelling, tasting)— is also hierarchical and occurs in stages. The sensing pathways in particular develop during sensitive periods (mostly ages 0–3), linking with other biological pathways to affect learning, behavior, and health (both physical and mental) (figure 1.11).

Language development and language skills, which are precursors of critical thinking skills, emerge from a series of neurobiological transformations occurring in the early years of life. Language does not suddenly appear at some predetermined age in some predetermined fashion. Rather, it emerges after a child has begun to engage with his or her caregivers in interactive activities, such as sharing, requesting, imitating, playing, naming, and describing. Hart and Risley (1995) demonstrate that word accumulation begins very early in life; differences among children from different social groups are apparent at 36 months (with the differences correlating directly with differences in the amount of language between parent and child) (figure 1.12). Differences in verbal skills continue—along trajectories—and are still present at age 9.

Research on the brain indicates that a child's early environment shapes school readiness (Smith, Fairchild, and Groginsky 1997; Shonkoff and Phillips 2000). Academic performance in later years also correlates with exposure to early interventions. In their 1992 analysis of eighth graders'

Figure 1.11   Sensitive Periods of Brain Development

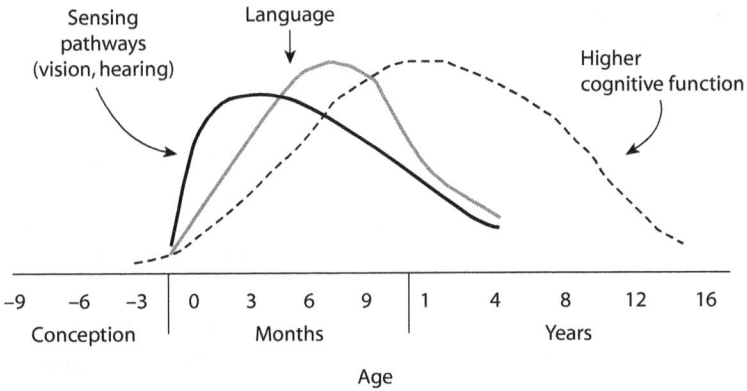

Source: Shonkoff 2000.

Figure 1.12   Effect of Family Talkativeness on Child's Vocabulary Through Age 3

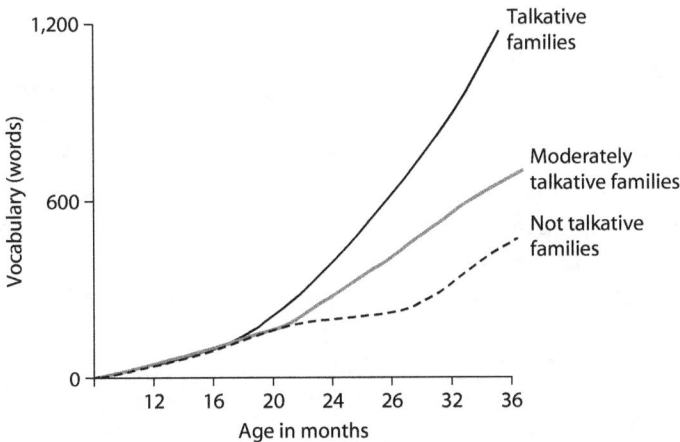

Source: Hart and Risley 1995.

performance on the mathematics test of the National Assessment of Educational Progress (NAEP), Fuchs and Reklis (1994) find that characteristics of children (for example, readiness to learn in kindergarten) and their households (for example, mother's education) had much larger effects on their NAEP test scores than did classroom variables (for example, staffing ratio).

Together, a child's environment and early learning experiences determine lifelong trajectories and abilities for learning, behavior, health, and ultimately productivity. Experience-based brain development lays the foundation for the full range of human competencies essential for true human capital formation.

The results of the OECD's Programme for International Student Assessment (PISA) (OECD 2010a), a cross-national comparison of mathematics, science, and reading skills of 15-year-olds, provides fresh evidence reaffirming the contribution of ECD to school readiness and subsequent achievement.[10] China participated in this international assessment for the first time, although only Shanghai took part (the sample is therefore not nationally representative). Shanghai had the highest scores among participating countries and territories.

There was a difference of more than 60 score points (about 10 percent of the difference in Shanghai's score) between students who had attended preprimary school for more than a year and students who had not (figure 1.13). In Israel, this difference was 120 points. The differences remain large even after accounting for socioeconomic background (Schleicher 2010).

Cognitive skills as well as noncognitive skills have a positive impact on economic development because they enhance the capacity to use, adopt, and generate technology and to innovate to solve problems. Differences in cognitive skills account for most of the differences in economic growth rates across OECD countries (Hanushek and Woessmann 2008, 2009; OECD 2010a). Hanushek and Kimko (2000) estimate that an increase of one country-level standard deviation in test performance yielded about a 1 percentage point increase in annual economic growth rates during the period 1960–90. Given the impact of ECD on subsequent academic achievement, investing in ECD can help boost student achievement, which, in turn, enhances a country's capacity to innovate and sustain competitiveness.

Economic Returns to Early Child Development
Inequitable access to ECD services has contributed to inequitable outcomes in health, educational attainment and achievement, lifetime

Figure 1.13   Differences in PISA Scores between 15-Year-Old Students Who Attended Preprimary School for at least One Year or and Those Who Did Not

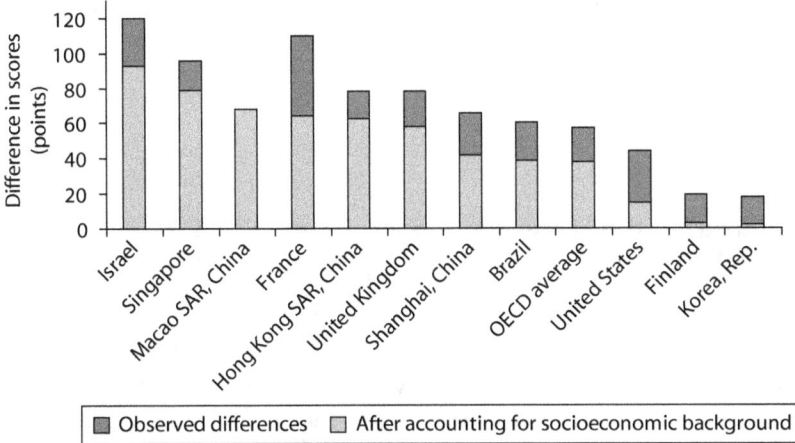

| Observed differences | After accounting for socioeconomic background |

Source: Schleicher 2010.
Note: PISA is the Programme for International Student Assessment.

earnings, and potentially disruptive social behavior. Carneiro and Heckman (2003) conclude that investing in ECD yields high economic returns because early learning is far more productive and cost-effective than later, remedial education, as the social and behavioral skills that children learn in their early years set a pattern for acquiring positive life skills later in life (box 1.3).

To analyze the economic impact of early child development programs, these researchers used cost-benefit analyses to convert the benefits and costs of these programs into monetary values in constant dollars discounted at a rate of 3–5 percent a year. They also measured the internal rate of return of these programs by estimating the time periods over which the costs and benefits in constant dollars were paid or received by program participants and society. The real internal rate of return of several carefully evaluated programs ranged from 7 to 18 percent— higher than the average returns to financial capital, which were less than 7 percent (table 1.2).

Table 1.3 presents the evaluation findings of the long-term impact of ECD programs in Argentina, Bangladesh, Colombia, Turkey, and the United States. Consistently, these interventions led to highly desirable outcomes:

children who participated exhibited greater motivation to learn, higher achievement, and greater self-esteem than children who did not.

Early intervention can also improve a child's prospects for successful employment later in life by fostering critical learning skills early in life.

Box 1.3

Measuring the Economic Impact of Early Child Development

James Heckman, a Nobel laureate in economics from the University of Chicago, has advocated forcefully for greater public funding for early child development programs. His work came out of his study of the retraining of steelworkers. When the steel industry in northwest Indiana began to decline, Heckman examined the economic impact of programs that provided job retraining for the steelworkers who would soon be forced to find employment elsewhere. His conclusions pointed to problems associated with teaching older workers new job skills and the high economic cost retraining workers who would soon retire. He concluded that "The returns to human capital investments are greatest for the young for two reasons: (a) skill begets skills and (b) younger people have a longer horizon over which to recoup the fruits of their investments" (Heckman 1999, p. 42).

In subsequent work, he and other researchers (Grunewald and Rolnick 2003; Schulman and Barnett 2005) used longitudinal cost-benefit analyses to argue that the economic gains for early childhood education are not reaped only by the children themselves but lead to significant gains for the overall economy. These researchers often cite the case of the Perry Preschool in Michigan, attended by children from low-income African-American families. For every $1 invested in the Perry School program during the early 1960s, more than $8 in benefits were returned to program participants and society as a whole (box figure 1.3.1). Participants in these programs benefited directly from their increase in after-tax earnings and fringe benefits; benefits also accrued to the general public. In fact, about 80 percent of the benefits of early child development programs went to the general public (students were less disruptive in class and went on to commit fewer crimes), yielding more than a 12 percent internal rate of return for society. Compared with other public investments—even those in the private sector—early childhood education appears to be extremely cost-effective.

(continued next page)

Box 1.3 *(continued)*

Box Figure 1.3.1   Rates of Return to Investments in Human Development in the United States

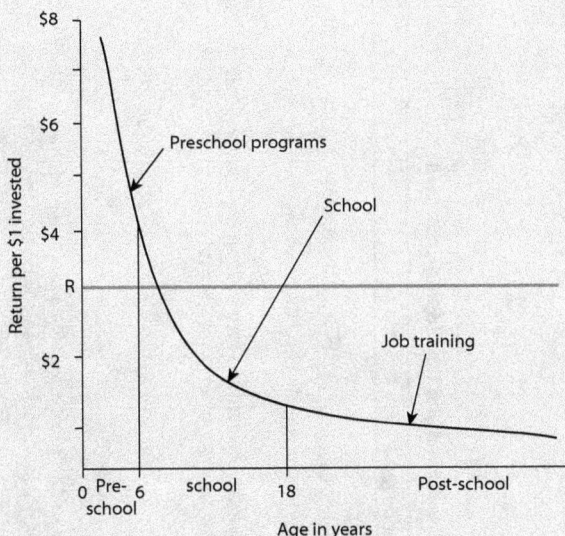

Source: Carneiro and Heckman 2003.

Table 1.2   Benefit-Cost Ratios of Three Preschool Programs in the United States

Program	Total benefit per child ($)	Total cost per child ($)	Net benefit per child ($)	Benefit/ cost ratio	Internal rate of return (%)
Michigan Perry Preschool (follow-up of participants at age 40) (2000 dollars)	244,811	15,166	99,682	16.1	18
Chicago Child Parent Center (1998 dollars)	47,759	6,692	41,067	7.1	10
Carolina Abecedarian (2002 dollars)	135,546	35,864	99,682	3.8	7

Source: Naudeau and others 2011.
Note: Benefits and cost were discounted at 3 percent.

Table 1.3 Impact of Selected Early Child Development Programs in Developed and Developing Countries

Country/program/content	Evaluation result
Argentina	
Preschool program	Participants increased average third grade test scores in math and Spanish by 8 percent compared with control group.
Bangladesh	
Center-based preschool education	Participants outperformed their peers in the control group by 58 percent on standardized test of school readiness.
Colombia	
Community-based comprehensive early child development interventions	Participants were twice as likely as control group to be enrolled in third grade.
Turkey	
Mother-child education program	Proportion of students who remained in school during adolescence was 86 percent for participants and 67 percent for control group.
United States	
Carolina Abecedarian	At ages 20 and 21, program participants were 2.7 times more likely to be attending a four-year college than control group.
Children from 6 weeks old to age 5 received early care and preschool services, with special curriculum focused on language development in small classes.	

Chicago Child-Parent Center
3- to 5-year-olds in high poverty areas attended three hours of preschool a day for a year and received reading and mathematics instruction from well-qualified teachers in small classes.

Perry Preschool, Michigan
In the 1960s, 3- to 4-year-olds in high poverty areas were provided 2.5 hours a day of instruction a day during the week and a 1.5 hour home visit once a week for a year. Teachers were certified to teach in elementary, early childhood, and special education and were paid 10 percent above the local public school district's standard pay scale. During the annual 30-week program, about one teacher was on staff for every six children.

Syracuse Preschool Program
Prenatal care and ECD services were provided to disadvantaged children through age 5.

At ages 20 and 21, program participants had 22 percent higher rate of high school graduation and 32 percent fewer juvenile arrests compared with control group.

At age 27, 117 of original 123 program participants were located and interviewed. During their elementary and secondary schooling, program participants were less likely to be placed in a special education program and had significantly higher average achievement scores than nonparticipants. More than 65 percent graduated from high school, compared with 45 percent of control group. Four times as many participants as nonparticipants earned $2,000 or more a month. The number of arrests was one-fifth that of nonparticipants. At age 41, participants were 25 percent less likely to be on welfare than the control group. Ten years later problems with probation and criminal offenses were 70 percent less among participants than among control group.

Source: Naudeau and others 2011.

By the time children enter school, their early development will have determined whether they will succeed in school and later in life; the extent of their learning in school and throughout life depends largely on the social and emotional competence they develop in their early years (Carnegie Corporation 1996). Children who are ready for school share a combination of positive characteristics: they are socially engaged and emotionally stable, confident, friendly, and attentive; have good peer relationships; tackle and persist with challenging tasks; have good language and communication skills; and listen to instructions.

ECD programs have both broad and specific effects on the development of human capital. Although poor children tend to be more vulnerable than other children, there is no definitive cut-off point between children below a certain poverty line and those above that poverty line. Rather, there is a gradient of risks, which lasts a lifetime (figure 1.14).

Neglecting ECD imposes a high opportunity cost on both children and society. To build a harmonious society, China must eliminate absolute poverty and reduce inequality. Eventually ensuring that all children can grow up to live to their full potential will both improve the quality of human development and enhance China's competitiveness.

Figure 1.14   Academic Abilities of Kindergartners, by Household Income, United States

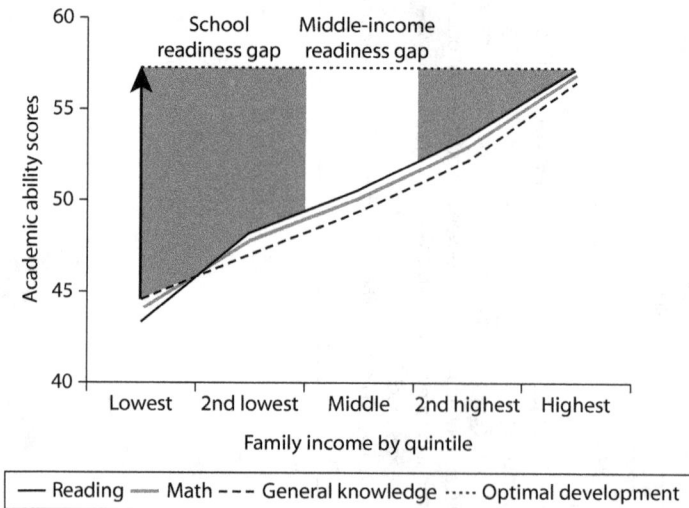

Source: Schulman and Barnett 2005.

Annex 1A Key Educational Indicators in China and Conceptual Framework for Early Child Development

Table 1A.1   Key Educational Indicators in China and Selected Economy Groups, 2009

Indicator	China	East Asia and Pacific	High-income economies	Middle-income economies
Education inputs				
Public education expenditure as percentage of GDP	3.5	3.5	5.8 (OECD)	4.3
Primary school pupil-teacher ratio	18	20	14	24
Gross enrollment ratio (%)				
Preprimary	51	42	78	44
Primary education (grades 1–6)	106	106	101	111
Secondary education (grades 7–12)	99 (junior-secondary), 79 (senior-secondary and technical and vocational education)	73	—	70
Higher education (vocational colleges and universities)	24	21	67	24
Adult literacy rate (%)				
Men	96	96	99	90
Women	90	90	99	80

Source: World Bank Edstat.
Note: — = not available.

Figure 1A.1   Conceptual Framework for Child Development From Birth to Age 6

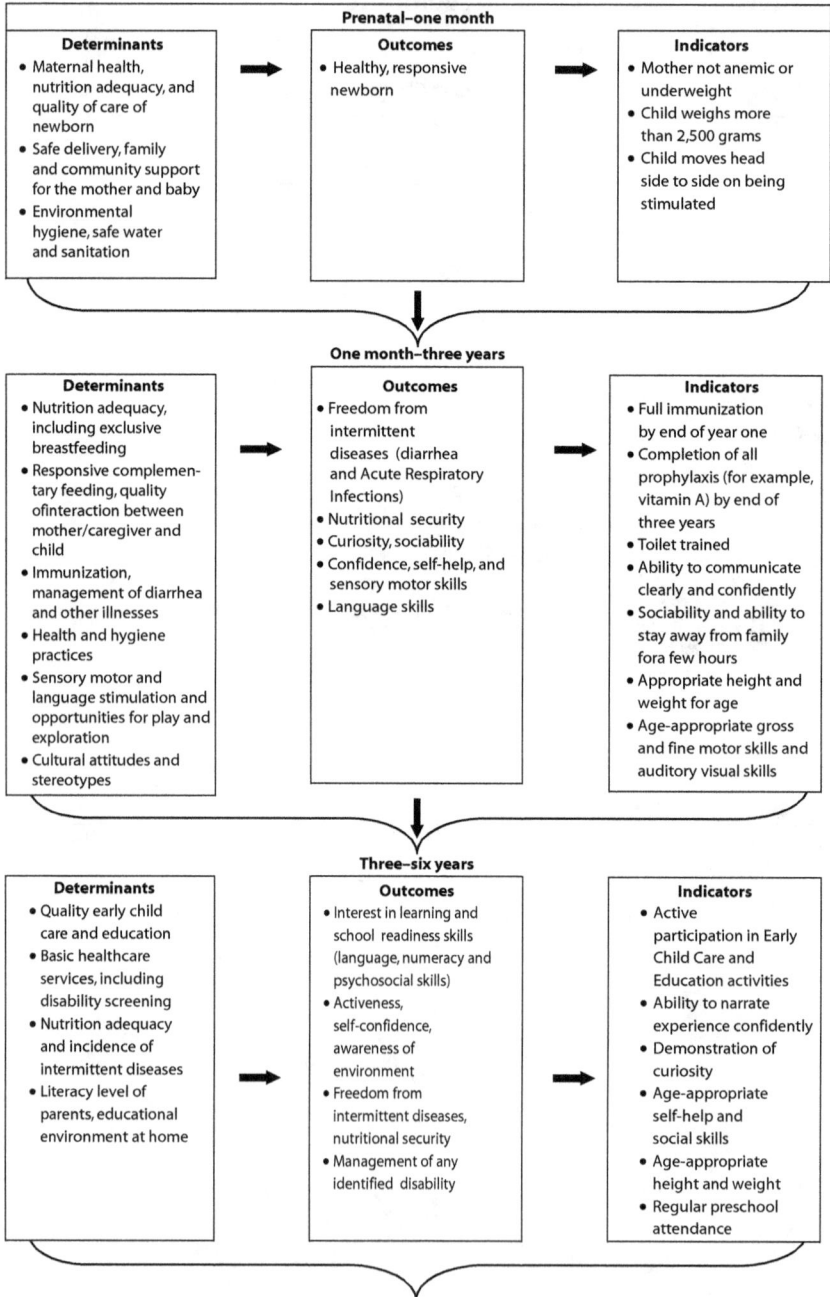

Prenatal–one month

Determinants	**Outcomes**	**Indicators**
• Maternal health, nutrition adequacy, and quality of care of newborn • Safe delivery, family and community support for the mother and baby • Environmental hygiene, safe water and sanitation	• Healthy, responsive newborn	• Mother not anemic or underweight • Child weighs more than 2,500 grams • Child moves head side to side on being stimulated

One month–three years

Determinants	**Outcomes**	**Indicators**
• Nutrition adequacy, including exclusive breastfeeding • Responsive complementary feeding, quality of interaction between mother/caregiver and child • Immunization, management of diarrhea and other illnesses • Health and hygiene practices • Sensory motor and language stimulation and opportunities for play and exploration • Cultural attitudes and stereotypes	• Freedom from intermittent diseases (diarrhea and Acute Respiratory Infections) • Nutritional security • Curiosity, sociability • Confidence, self-help, and sensory motor skills • Language skills	• Full immunization by end of year one • Completion of all prophylaxis (for example, vitamin A) by end of three years • Toilet trained • Ability to communicate clearly and confidently • Sociability and ability to stay away from family for a few hours • Appropriate height and weight for age • Age-appropriate gross and fine motor skills and auditory visual skills

Three–six years

Determinants	**Outcomes**	**Indicators**
• Quality early child care and education • Basic healthcare services, including disability screening • Nutrition adequacy and incidence of intermittent diseases • Literacy level of parents, educational environment at home	• Interest in learning and school readiness skills (language, numeracy and psychosocial skills) • Activeness, self-confidence, awareness of environment • Freedom from intermittent diseases, nutritional security • Management of any identified disability	• Active participation in Early Child Care and Education activities • Ability to narrate experience confidently • Demonstration of curiosity • Age-appropriate self-help and social skills • Age-appropriate height and weight • Regular preschool attendance

Source: World Bank 2004.

Notes

1. In current prices, China's per capita GDP in 2010 reached RMB29,992 (about $4,476), according to the *China Statistical Yearbook 2011.*

2. China's 12th Five-Year Plan (2011–15) aims to increase average life expectancy to 74.5 years by 2015.

3. The NER and GER are statistical measures used in the education sector. According to the UNESCO Institute of Statistics, the NER is enrollment of the official age group for a given level of education, expressed as a percentage of the corresponding population; the GER is total enrollment within a country for a specific level of education, regardless of age, expressed as a percentage of the population in the official age group corresponding to the level of education. The GER can exceed 100 percent when the number of students enrolled includes underage and overage students for a given grade level.

4. The Chinese education system comprises preprimary education (for children 2–6); primary education (grades 1–6, for children ages 6 or 7–11 or 12); junior-secondary education (grades 7–9, for children ages 12–14); senior-secondary education (grades 10–12, for young people ages 15–17), and higher education (which includes postsecondary colleges and degree-granting universities). Compulsory education covers grades 1–9.

5. The Gini coefficient for the United States was 0.467 in 2010 (U.S. Census Bureau 2011a).

6. The exchange rate used ($1 = RMB6.2787) was as of April 27, 2012.

7. By comparison, the official poverty rate in the United States in 2010 was 15.1 percent (U.S. Census Bureau 2011b).

8. Under-5 mortality—the probability of dying before the age of 5—is a leading indicator of the level of child health and overall development in countries. It is also a Millennium Development Goal indicator.

9. About 70 percent of China's population has agricultural resident status (*hukou*), but only 55 percent of the population actually lives in rural areas, because about 211 million Chinese are migrant workers from rural areas. The difference between the urbanization rate (45 percent) and the percentage of agricultural *hukou* reflects rural to urban migration. Migrant workers' children are counted as rural residents.

10. The PISA is an international assessment by the OECD of achievement in mathematics, science, and reading by 15-year-olds in both member and nonmember states. Started in 2000, the international assessments are conducted every three years to inform policy and practices in education. The 2009 assessment tested 470,000 students in 65 countries in 2009 and another 50,000 students in 9 countries in 2010. The municipality of Shanghai (with a population of 20 million people) participated for the first time, placing first in all three areas.

References

Alderman, H., ed. 2011. *No Small Matter: The Impact of Poverty, Shocks, and Human Capital Investments in Early Childhood Development.* Washington, DC: World Bank.

All-China Women's Federation, National Population and Family Planning Commission, Ministry of Education, Ministry of Civil Affairs, Ministry of Health, Civilization Office of the Central Communist Party Committee, and China National Committee for the Well-Being of Youth. 2010. *National Guidelines on Family Education.* Beijing (中华全国妇女联合会、国家人口和计划生育委员会、教育部、民政部、卫生部、中央文明办、中国关心下一代工作委员会。全国家庭教育指导大纲)

Carnegie Corporation. 1996. *Years of Promise; A Comprehensive Learning Strategy for America's Children.* Report of the Carnegie Task Force on Learning in the Primary Grades. New York: Carnegie Corporation.

Carneiro, P., and J. Heckman. 2003. "Human Capital Policy." NBER Working Paper 9495, National Bureau of Economic Research, Cambridge, MA. http://www.nber.org/papers/w9495.

Chen, J. S. 2009. Presentation of findings from *Report of China Food and Nutrition Surveillance System 2009*, International Symposium on Anti-Poverty and Early Childhood Development, Beijing, October 29–30.

China Daily. 2010. "China's Wealth Divide Past Warning Level." http://www.chinadaily.com/china/2010-05/12.

———. 2011a. "The Journey towards Longer Life." http://www.chinadaily.com/china/2011-4/28.

———. 2011b. "China's Sex Ratio Declines for 2 Straight Years." http://www.chinadaily.com/china/2011-08/16.

Ellis, B. J., J. J. Jackson, and W. T. Boyce. 2006. "The Stress Response Systems: Universality and Adaptive Individual Differences." *Developmental Review* 26: 175–212.

Ferreira, F., and J. Gignoux. 2007. *Inequality of Economic Opportunity in Latin America.* Development Research Group. Washington, DC: World Bank

Fuchs, V., and D. Reklis. 1994. "Mathematical Achievement in Eighth Grade: Interstate and Racial Differences." NBER Working Paper 4784, National Bureau of Economic Research, Cambridge, MA.

Grunewald, R., and A. Rolnick. 2003. "Early Childhood Development: Economic Development with a High Public Return." *Fedgazette* (March), Federal Reserve Bank of Minneapolis.

Hanushek, E. A., and D. D. Kimko. 2000. "Schooling, Labour Force Quality, and the Growth of Nations." *American Economic Review* 90 (5): 1184–208.

Hanushek, E. A., and L. Woessmann. 2008. "The Role of Cognitive Skills in Economic Development." *Journal of Economic Literature* 46 (3): 607–68.

———. 2009. "Do Better Schools Lead to More Growth? Cognitive Skills, Economic Outcomes, and Causation." NBER Working Paper 14633, National Bureau of Economic Research, Cambridge, MA.

Hart, B., and T. R. Risley. 1995. *Meaningful Differences in the Everyday Experiences of Young American Children.* Baltimore, MD: Paul H. Brookes Publishing Company.

Heckman, J. 1999. "Policies to Foster Human Capital." NBER Working Paper 7288, National Bureau of Economic Research, Cambridge, MA.

———. 2000. "Invest in the Very Young." Ounce of Prevention Fund, Chicago, IL.

Keating, D. P. 2011. "Society and Early Child Development: Developmental Health Disparities in the Nature-and-Nurture Paradigm." In *Nature and Nurture in Early Child Development*, ed. D. P. Keating [pp 245–291]. New York: Cambridge University Press.

McCain, M. N., J. F. Mustard, and K. McCuaig. 2011. *Early Years Study 3: Making Decisions, Taking Actions.* Toronto: Margaret & Wallace McCain Family Foundation.

MOE (Ministry of Education). Various years. *Educational Statistics Yearbook of China.* Department of Development and Planning. Beijing: People's Education Press. (教育部发展计划司。中国教育统计年鉴。中国教育出版社。北京)

MOH (Ministry of Health). 2009. *China Health Statistics Yearbook.* Beijing: China Xiehe Medical University Press. (卫生部。中国卫生统计年鉴。中国协和医科大学出版社。北京)

———. 2011. "Statistics on Health Development in 2011." Center for Statistics Information, Beijing. http://www.moh.gov.cn/publicfiles/business/htmfiles. (卫生部。统计信息中心。2011年卫生发展统计。北京)

Mustard, J. F. 2007. "Experience-Based Brain Development: Scientific Underpinnings of the Importance of Early Child Development in a Global World." In *Early Child Development: From Measurement to Action. A Priority for Growth and Equity*, ed. M. E. Young, 35–64. Washington, DC: World Bank. http://www.worldbank.org/children/ECDtoHuman Development.pdf.

National Scientific Council on the Developing Child. 2007. "A Science-Based Framework for Early Childhood Policy: Using Evidence to Improve Outcomes in Learning, Behavior, and Health for Vulnerable Children." Center on the Developing Child, Harvard University, Cambridge, MA. http://www.developingchild.harvard.edu.

Naudeau, S., N. Kataoka, A. Valario, M. J. Neuman, and L. K. Elder. 2011. *Investing in Young Children: An Early Childhood Development Guide for Policy Dialogue and Project Preparation*. Directions in Development. Washington, DC: World Bank.

NBS (National Bureau of Statistics of China). 2009a. *Poverty Monitoring of Rural China*. Beijing: China Statistics Press. (国家统计局。中国农村减贫监测报告.中国统计出版社。北京)

———. 2009b. *China Statistical Yearbook*. Beijing: China Statistics Press. (国家统计局。中国统计年鉴。中国统计出版社。北京)

———. 2009c. *China Population and Employment Statistics Yearbook*. Department of Population and Employment Statistics. Beijing: China Statistics Press. (国家统计局。中国人口和就业统计年鉴。中国统计出版社。北京)

———. 2011. *China Statistical Yearbook*. Beijing: China Statistics Press.

Nelson, C. 2000. "The Developing Brain." In *From Neurons to Neighborhoods: The Science of Early Child Development*, ed. J. P. Shonkoff and D. A. Phillips [pp183-217]. Washington, DC: National Academy Press.

NPC (National People's Congress), and CPPCC (Chinese People's Political Consultative Conference). 2011. *Outline of the Twelfth Five-Year Plan of Economic and Social Development of China*. Beijing: NPC and CPPCC. http://www.gov.cn/2011h/content_1825838.htm. (全国人民代表大会和中国人民政治协商会议。中国国民经济和社会发展第十二个五年规划纲要)

NPFPC (National Population and Family Planning Commission). 2010. *Chinese Migrant Population Report 2010*. Beijing: NPFPC. www.chinapop.gov.cn/xwzx/xwyw/2010006/t20100626_208390. (国家人口和计划生育委员会。中国流动人口报告。北京)

OECD (Organisation for Economic Co-operation and Development). Various years. *Education at a Glance*. Paris: OECD.

———. 2010a. *The High Cost of Low Educational Performance: The Long-Run Economic Impact of Improving PISA Outcomes*. Paris: OECD.

OECD family database. http://www.oecd.org/dataoecd/46/13/37864698.pdf

Schleicher, A. 2010. Presentation on Programme for International Student Assessment (PISA) before U.S. Congress in Washington DC on December 7, 2010. http://pisa2009.acer.edu.au/.

Schulman, K., and W. S. Barnett. 2005. "The Benefits of Prekindergarten for Middle-Income Children." NIEER Policy Report, National Institute for Early Education Research, Rutgers University, New Brunswick, NJ.

Shonkoff, J. P., and D. A. Phillips. 2000. *From Neurons to Neighborhoods: The Science of Early Child Development*. Washington, DC: National Academy Press.

Smith, S., M. Fairchild, and S. Groginsky. 1997. *Early Childhood Care and Education: An Investment that Works*, 2nd ed. Denver, CO: National Conference of State Legislatures.

State Council. 2011a. *Development of the Elderly in the 12th Five-Year Plan.* Number 28. http://www.gov.cn/zwgk/2011-09/23. (国务院。中国老龄事业发展"十二五"规划)

———. 2011b. *Guidelines on Chinese Women Development (2011–2020)* and *Guidelines on Chinese Children Development (2011–2020).* No. 24. Beijing: State Council. http://www.gov.cn/2011-08/08. (国务院。中国妇女发展纲要 (2011–2020)。 中国儿童发展纲要 (2011–2020))

UN (United Nations). Millennium Development Goals. http://www.un.org/mil lenniumgoals.

United Nations Interagency Group for Estimation of Child Mortality. 2011. *Levels & Trends in Child Mortality, Report 2011.* New York: United Nations Children's Fund. http://www.childinfo.org/files/Child_Mortality_Report 2011.

U.S. Census Bureau. 2011a. *Household Income for States: 2009 and 2010.* Washington, DC: U.S. Census Bureau. http://www.census.gov/prod/2011pubs.

———. 2011b. *Income, Poverty, and Health Insurance Coverage in the United States: 2010.* Washington, DC: U.S. Census Bureau. http://www.census.gov/prod/2011pubs.

Wang, Rong, and Wu Kin Bing. 2008. "Urban Service Delivery and Governance in Education in Five Chinese Cities." Draft. East Asia Human Development Department. World Bank, Washington, DC.

WHO (World Health Organization). 2011. *World Health Statistics.* http://www .who.int/whosis/whostat/2011.

World Bank. 2004. *Reaching Out to the Child: An Integrated Approach to Child Development.* Human Development Sector, South Asia Region. Washington, DC: World Bank.

———. 2009a. "China Education Sector Review: Inputs and Suggestions to China's National Plan for Medium- and Long-Term Educational Reform and Development." Draft. East Asia Human Development Department. World Bank, Washington, DC.

———. 2009b. "China Rural Compulsory Education Finance Reform: A Case Study of Gansu." Draft. East Asia Human Development Department. World Bank, Washington, DC.

———. 2010. "World Bank Inputs to China's 12th Five-Year Plan." Draft. China Country Management Unit. World Bank, Washington, DC.

World Bank database. http://data.worldbank.org/indicator/SE.PRE.ENPR

Xie, Q., and M. E. Young. 1999. "Integrated Child Development in Rural China." Human Development Network Education Unit. World Bank, Washington, DC.

Xinhua News. 2011. "China Raises Poverty Line by 80 Pct to Benefit over 100 Mln." news.xinhuanet.com/english2010/china/2011-11/29.

CHAPTER 2

Policy on and Challenges to Providing Early Child Development Services

China's policymakers have long recognized that young children represent the country's future. Between 1949 and 1965, the government introduced early child development (ECD) services in order to free up women to participate in the new society's labor force. Almost all government departments, enterprises, and agricultural collectives operated nurseries and kindergartens for their staff.[1] Although kindergartens were shut down during the Cultural Revolution (1966–76), the introduction of economic reform in 1978 ushered in the expansion of ECD services, as well as the introduction of various Western child-centered educational theories (Dewey, Montessori, Bronfenbrenner, Bruner, Piaget, and Vyotsky). A series of administrative directives and laws were passed to ensure young children's survival, protection, development, and education. This chapter examines the legal framework, the policy and administrative structure, and the structure of service delivery of ECD services.

Legal Framework and Recent Policies

China's early childhood services are guided by laws approved by the People's Congress and by regulations and guidelines set forth by the

State Council. Table 2.1 lists the major ones relevant to the operation of these services.

The *Law on Protection of Minors*, promulgated in 1991 and amended in 2006, streamlined the responsibilities of local governments at various levels to integrate the protection of minors into the national economic and social development plans and annual plans; increase fiscal support; operate kindergartens and nurseries; and promote home-based services by state and social organizations, enterprises, and individuals.

Table 2.1   Major Laws, Regulations, and Guidelines on Protection and Development of Children in China, 1985–2011

Law, regulation, or guideline	Date passed or promulgated
Health Regime in Nurseries and Kindergartens	December 1985
Regulations on Kindergartens	August 1989
Law on Protection of Minors	Promulgated in September 1991, amended in December 2006
Law on Maternal and Infant Care	October 1994
Regulations on the Management of Health and Hygiene in Nurseries and Kindergartens	December 1994
Education Law	March 1995
Regulations on the Qualifications and Responsibilities of Kindergarten Directors	January 1996
Guidelines for Kindergarten Education	August 2001
Guidelines Governing the Reform and Development of the Early Childhood Education	January 2003
National Guidelines on the Safety and Standards of Children's Toys	2003
Regulations on the Safety Management in Primary and Secondary Schools and Kindergartens	June 2006
The National Guidelines on Family Education	February 2010
China's National Plan Outline for Medium- and Long-Term Reform and Development of Education (2010–2020)	July 2010
Guidelines on the Development of Preprimary Education	November 2010
The 12th Five-Year Plan of National Economic and Social Development of the People's Republic of China (2011–2015)	March 2011
Guidelines on Chinese Women's Development (2011–2020)	July 2011
Guidelines on Chinese Children Development (2011–2020)	July 2011
Population Development Plan in the 12th Five-Year Plan (2011–2015)	November 2011
Guidelines on Poverty Reduction and the Development of Chinese Rural Areas (2011–2020)	December 2011

Sources: UNICEF 2007; Dai 2009; State Council 2010a, 2010b, 2011b, 2011c, 2011d; NPC and CPPCC 2011.

In 1989 and 1996, the State Council approved two documents governing kindergartens. The first, *the Regulations on Kindergartens*, is the legal basis for operating kindergarten services. These regulations set specific norms and standards for preschool education, including language, basic activities, health and hygiene, and safety. The second, *the Regulations on the Management of Kindergartens*, sets forth the principles of operation of kindergartens. These regulations establish comprehensive norms and standards for utilization of space, class size, hygiene and health, safety, qualification requirements of kindergarten personnel, and the relationships among the family, community, and kindergarten.

At the beginning of the 21st century, the State Council issued major documents to guide implementation of policy on ECD, namely, the *Guidelines for Kindergarten Education* (August 2001) and the *Guidelines Governing the Reform and Development of the Early Childhood Education* (January 2003). The *Guidelines* establish the framework for provision of formal and nonformal ECDE services, led by the government, with participation of nongovernment sectors. A network of community-based, ECD service centers is to be developed around demonstration kindergartens and is to cater to the diverse needs of rural and urban areas. The *Guidelines* define the responsibilities of various levels of government, an accountability system, and the basic standards for investment, teachers, and overall quality of kindergartens. It recommends flexible methods for overcoming regional and rural-urban disparities and an integrated approach that blends parental and formal services (Corter and others 2006).

The 11th Conference of China's National People's Congress (NPC) and Chinese People's Political Consultative Conference (CPPCC) put unprecedented emphasis on improving the livelihood of the people and social development, with the ultimate goal of transforming China from a "large, populous country" to a "country with strong human resources" that is competitive in the global economy. A series of mutually reinforcing and cross-referenced guidelines on human development and poverty reduction, with a focus on children, women, and the family, were promulgated in support of this policy:

- The *National Guidelines on Family Education* (2010)—issued jointly by the All-China Women's Federation, the National Population and Family Planning Commission (NPFPC), the Ministry of Education, the Ministry of Civil Affairs, the Ministry of Health, the Civilization Office of the Central Communist Party Committee, and the China National Committee for the Well-being of Youth— reflects a heightened awareness of the family as a foundation for nation building.

- *China's National Plan Outline for Medium- and Long-Term Education Reform and Development (2010–2020)* (henceforth the *Educational Plan*) set targets for expansion of preprimary education for the next decade (State Council 2010a) (see annex table 5A.2).[2]
- The *Guidelines on the Development of Preprimary Education* (State Council 2010b) provide concrete suggestions about how to expand preprimary education, including instructing various levels of governments to coordinate planning, ensure the age-appropriateness of kindergarten curriculum, and integrate expenditures into the budget to ensure that the mandate is funded (see annex table 5A.3).
- *The 12th Five-Year Plan* (2011–2015) (NPC and CPPCC 2011), which provided the guiding principles and specific direction in all sectors for a five year period, reaffirmed the principles of improving people's livelihood and social integration in its social and economic policies.
- The *Guidelines on Chinese Women Development (2011–2020), the Guidelines on Chinese Children Development (2011–2020), the Guidelines on Poverty Reduction and Development of Chinese Rural Areas (2011–2020), and the Plan for Population Development in the 12th Five-Year Plan* (State Council 2011b, 2011c, 2011d) propose goals and targets; multisectoral interventions that cover health, education, social protection, and law; assign responsibilities to government agencies; integrate expenditures into the regular budget to ensure the mandate is funded; and identify indicators and evaluation criteria in the development in these areas. These call for tighter intersectoral coordination. The multipronged approach within and across these sectors reinforces the principles of gender equality, protection of children's rights, development of children ages 0–6, and support for disadvantaged children (including those who are left behind in rural areas, orphans, children with special needs, poor children, rural children, and children of ethnic minorities) (see annex tables 5A.4–5A.6).

These implementation-oriented guidelines and plans herald a new era of human development, within which ECD will play a key role in breaking the cycle of poverty and increasing social cohesion and future competitiveness. In 2011, resource allocation was made in support of the new policy direction. Prenatal care and hospital delivery were made free for women in rural areas, and RMB50 billion ($7.9 billion) was allocated to support the expansion of preprimary education under the 12th Five-Year Plan period (State Council 2011e). Another RMB16 billion ($2.5 billion) was allocated annually to support free school meals for students in compulsory education in the Western and Central areas (MOE 2011b).

Policy and Administration

To implement these progressive policies, China has to overcome major challenges associated with the diffusion of policy, coordination, administration, finance, and service delivery in ECD. Diverse entities operate early childhood programs, including public and private organizations, multiple government sectors, and national and local departments. The National Working Committee for Children and Women under the State Council is the highest body coordinating responsibilities across ministries. It leads the development, monitoring, and implementation of the National Plan of Actions for Children and the National Plan of Actions for Women and is increasingly engaged in child development and welfare.

Policy and supervision are the responsibilities of line ministries; service provision and financing are primarily the responsibilities of county governments in rural areas and district governments in municipalities. Provincial and municipal governments exercise oversight of service delivery and often operate and finance training institutions.

Service provision to young children crosses several sectors, complicating the provision of seamless service to children and parents. There is insufficient regular coordination among stakeholders in ECD service standards, planning, and provision at the national and local levels.

The key service providers include the following institutions:

- Services to children under age 3 are provided mainly by the health sector. The Ministry of Health sets policy, organizes maternal and child health services, and monitors outcomes. It promulgates regulations on health and hygiene in nurseries and kindergartens and guides and monitors related work. The services provided by the health departments in local governments include prenatal and postnatal care, free vaccination, and free annual checkups for children (laboratory tests are not free).
- The Ministry of Human Resources and Labor Security defines occupational standards for workers caring for children ages 0–3, provides in-service training, and certifies them.

- The National Population and Family Planning Commission is responsible for raising the capability of the population. Its mandate extends from family planning to development of children from birth to age 3. It has established about 50 demonstration centers that provide services for maternal and child medical checkup and early stimulation (see box 3.1 in chapter 3 of this book for details).
- The Ministry of Education sets policy for and oversees the implementation of preprimary education for children ages 3–6, sets curricular standards, drafts laws and regulations, and monitors and evaluates preprimary education. Education departments at the provincial, municipal, county, and district levels operate and finance public kindergartens, approve and oversee private kindergartens, set the level of fees charged by public and private kindergartens, provide preservice and in-service teacher education, collect statistics, and inspect kindergartens.
- The Ministry of Civil Affairs considers ECD an integral part of community services. It has overall responsibilities for family welfare, child protection, and disaster relief. Local governments finance and operate orphanages for abandoned children and orphans.
- The All-China Women's Federation is the leading advocate of the rights of women and children. Through family education and development, it promotes the protection of these rights.
- The private sector, including nonprofit and for-profit organizations, operates about 68 percent of nurseries and kindergartens in China.

Table 2.2 details their responsibilities.

Structure of Service Delivery

Services for children under age 6 include pre- and postnatal care, nutrition and health, education, and family welfare.

Health

The Ministry of Health is responsible for crafting children's health care policies, planning development, and setting and implementing technical specifications and standards. Maternal and child health agencies fall under the jurisdiction of the Ministry of Health and a three-tiered network of maternal and child health centers. Under the technical guidance of county maternal and child health centers, township hospitals, village

Table 2.2 Policy, Administration, Finance, and Service Provision of Early Child Development in China

Institution	Policy, guidelines, and services	Training of providers	Finance	Point of service delivery
Ministry of Health	Sets health and hygiene standards in nurseries, kindergartens, and pre-schools; monitors maternal and child health; provides prenatal care, immuni-zation, well child checkups and sick child medical care for children ages 0–6	Provides preservice education of students at medical universities, trains other health workers in vocational schools	County and district govern-ments allocate own budgets; hospitals collect fees and generate other extrabudget-ary resources	Operates county and district hospitals, township clinics, and village health outposts
Ministry of Education	Sets policy and plans for preschool education (mostly for children 3–6); defines responsibilities at various government levels; provides guidelines for kindergarten and preschool education; provides education and certification of kindergarten principals and teachers	Provides preservice education of ECD teachers in specialized secondary schools, tertiary institutions, and universities	County and district govern-ments allocate own budgets; schools collect fees and gen-erate other extrabudgetary resources	Operates preschool classes attached to primary schools in villages and towns and kindergartens in cities and towns
Ministry of Human Resources and Social Security	Sets occupational standards for, educates, and certifies caregivers of children ages 0–3	Provides preservice education of caregivers of children ages 0–3 in vocational schools	County and district govern-ments allocate own budgets; schools collect fees and gen-erate other extrabudgetary resources	Operates vocational schools that train caregivers

(continued next page)

Table 2.2 (continued)

Institution	Policy, guidelines, and services	Training of providers	Finance	Point of service delivery
Ministry of Civil Affairs	Promotes ECD as part of community services; cares for orphans ages 0–15; provides adoption services, promotes child protection	Educates social workers	County and district governments allocate own budgets; orphanages collect fees from adoptive parents and generate extrabudgetary resources	Operates orphanages
National Population and Family Planning Commission	Is responsible for improving the capability of the population; promotes early child development; operates demonstration centers to promote early stimulation	Educates family planning cadres in specialized schools and provides them with in-service training to improve their ability to provide ECD	County and district governments allocate own budget; centers collect fees and generate other extrabudgetary resources	Operates early stimulation centers in county towns; operates demonstration centers
All-China Federation of Women	Advocates for the rights of women and children; supports family education; promotes community-based ECD services	Provides in-service training to local representatives of the All-China Women's Federation	County and district governments allocate own budgets; centers collect fees and generate other extrabudgetary resources	Operates community centers in county towns
NGOs and for-profit organizations	Serves the needs of children 2–6	Provides in-service training to ECD caregivers	Collects fees from users	Operate child care centers in cities and towns

Sources: Authors, based on interviews with officials at various ministries.

health clinics, and other medical and health institutions are responsible for providing child health services to the local community.

Following the Chinese National Children's Health Standard set by the Ministry of Health, newborns receive vaccinations and health assessments before discharge from the delivery hospital. In principle, maternal and child health professionals conduct regular health checkups for children ages 0–6, including two home visits for new-borns; four checkups during the first year of life; two checkups a year for 1- and 2-year-olds; and one checkup a year for children ages 3–6. This schedule is known as 2:4:2:1. Children have to be taken to clinics to receive these services. During checkups, qualified child health care professionals are supposed to provide immunizations (table 2.3), monitor growth, and provide basic health services, including guidance on feeding, nutrition, oral hygiene, communicable disease prevention, and health education and promotion. Table 2.3 provides the schedule of vaccination for children ages 0–6.

Health checkups had been fee based, especially for children ages 3–6, except for immunizations, which are free of charge. In recent years, in order to promote good health, some cities and provinces have started providing free health checkups for children ages 0–6 covering some basic items such as growth and hearing monitoring, dental health, and hemo-globin level tests. For children in grades 1–9, annual checkups are pro-vided at school at a nominal cost; they do not include laboratory tests.

Table 2.3   Vaccination Schedule for Children, Ages 0–6

Type	Age	Vaccine	Diseases prevented
Basic	At birth	Bacillus Calmette-Guérin (BCG), hepatitis B	Tuberculosis, hepatitis B
	1 month	Hepatitis B	Hepatitis B
	2 months	Oral polio vaccine (OPV)	Polio
Basic	3 months	Encephalitis	Encephalitis (brain inflammation)
	4 months	Diphtheria, pertussis, and tetanus (DPT)	Diphtheria, whooping cough, and tetanus (DPT)
	5 months	DPT	DPT
	6 months	Hepatitis B	Hepatitis B
	8 months	Measles	Measles
Booster	1.5 years	Encephalitis	Encephalitis
	4 years	Encephalitis, measles	Encephalitis, measles
	7 years	DPT	DPT

Source: Dai 2009, updated by Dr. Chaoying Liu of the World Bank in 2010.

Development and Education

Children under age 6 in China are cared for and educated in three types of institutions (see box 1.1 in chapter 1). Table 2.4 summarizes the types of health and education services offered to these children.

In 2008, about 48 percent of enrollment in preprimary education in rural areas was in one-year preschool classes, not in two or three-year kindergartens (figure 2.1). By contrast, preschool classes accounted for only 13 percent of ECD enrollment in cities and 25 percent in county towns. Urban children thus have a much earlier start in ECD, entering at age 2, 3, or 4 and staying on until they begin primary school. Rural children, if they have any access to ECD services, are more likely to start at age 5 or 6, giving them just one year of preparation before entering primary school. As a result, the school readiness of rural children is lower than that of urban children. Their late start puts them on a lower trajectory in school achievement, with long-term negative impact on education attainment, employment choice, and lifetime earnings.

The expansion of enrollment in kindergartens in the last two decades was driven largely by the growth of these services in cities, which masked the decline in service provision to rural areas. Between 1986 and 2010, the number of rural kindergartens was reduced by half, from 130,030 to 71,588, while the number of kindergartens grew from 24,500 to 35,845 in cities and from 18,700 to 42,987 in county towns (figure 2.2).

Enrollment (number of students) followed a similar pattern (figure 2.3). Between 1986 and 2010, enrollment in city kindergartens more than

Table 2.4   Early Child Development Services Provided in China

Age group/size of cohort	Type of service	Coverage
0–3 (~48 million)	Pre- and postnatal care; delivery; vaccination; medical checkups	99% immunized
	Cared for at home	90%
	Informal, home-based care	~5% in informal centers
	Nurseries and kindergartens, parent-child classes	~5% in formal institutions
3–6 (~51 million)	Kindergartens (2–3 years before primary school)	Gross enrollment ratio (GER) three years before primary school: 51% GER two years before primary school: 65%
	Preschool classes (1 year before primary school)	GER one year before primary school: 74%

Source: Authors' estimates based on statistics published in MOE and MOH statistical yearbooks.
Note: Only vaccinations are provided free of charge.

Figure 2.1   Enrollment in One-Year Preschool Classes as a Percentage of Total Enrollment in Kindergartens in Cities, County Towns, and Rural Areas of China, by Province, 2008

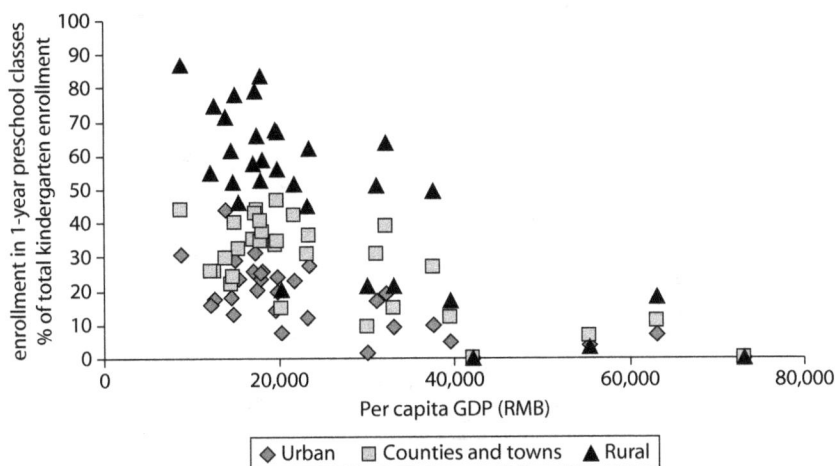

Source: MOE 2009.
Note: Figure includes public and private institutions.

doubled, from 3.6 million to 7.5 million, while enrollment in kindergartens in county towns rose from 2.2 million to 10.1 million. Enrollment in rural kindergartens fell from 10.5 million in 1986 to 9.4 million in 2003, although it gradually rose back to 12.1 million by 2010.

The number of rural teachers fell dramatically between 2000 and 2001, while the number of teachers in cities and towns increased sharply for the rest of the decade (figure 2.4). These changes raised the student-to-teacher ratio to 60:1 in rural areas in the early 2000s (it gradually trended down to 28:1 in 2010). By contrast, the student-to-teacher ratio in cities declined to 9:1 by 2010, and the ratio in towns fell to 16:1 (figure 2.5).

The decline in rural services in 1992 reflected the steep decline in government revenue that began with economic reform in 1978 (figure 2.6). Dismantling the planning apparatus led to erosion of the central government's main revenue mechanism—profits of state-owned enterprises—and drove the decentralization of expenditure. Although reform of the tax-sharing system in 1994 (through the introduction of a value added tax) enabled the central government's revenues to recover robustly a few years later, local governments continued to bear the main responsibilities of financing and providing basic educational services, including ECD.

Figure 2.2   Number of Kindergartens in China, 1986–2010

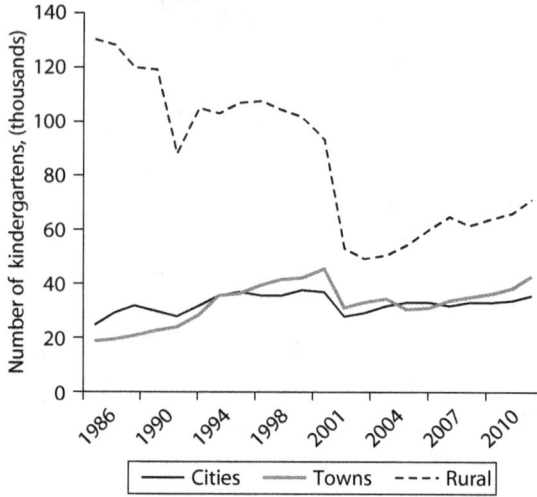

Source: MOE 2010.
Note: Figures include public and private institutions.

Figure 2.3   Number of Students in Kindergartens in China, 1986–2010

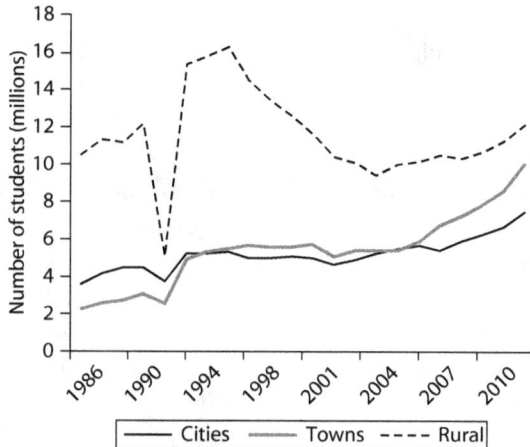

Source: MOE 2010.
Note: Figures include public and private institutions.

As fiscal capacity varies from locality to locality, so does the capacity for service provision. After 1994, revenues of subnational governments fell far short of expenditures. At the same time, as market reforms brought a major realignment of prices, the costs of providing public services rose

Figure 2.4   Number of Teachers in Kindergartens in China, 1997–2010

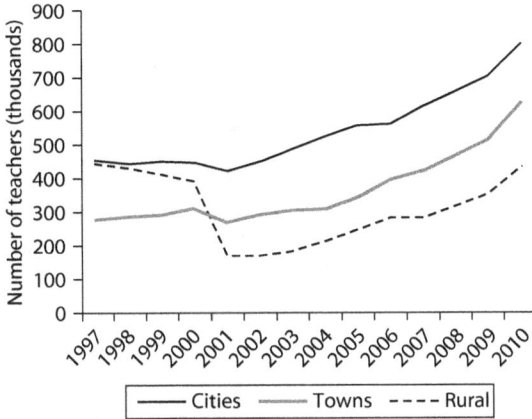

Source: MOE 2010.
Note: Figures include public and private kindergartens.

Figure 2.5   Number of Students per Teacher in Kindergartens, 1997–2010

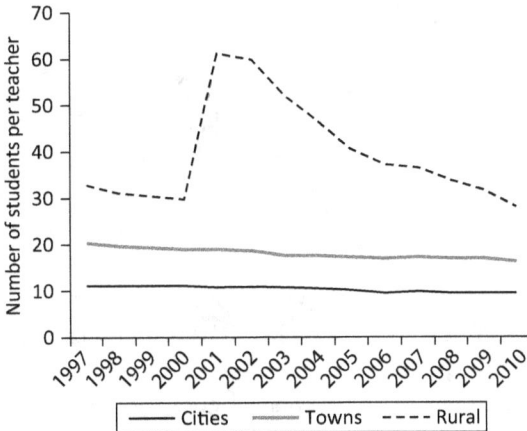

Source: MOE 2010.
Note: Figures include public and private kindergartens.

rapidly, adversely affecting service delivery in rural areas. In urban areas, increases in income led to rising demand for ECD services.

The student-to-teacher ratio is a good indicator of the quality of public kindergartens. In 2010, the student-to-teacher ratio ranged from 10:1 in Shanghai and Beijing to a staggering 94:1 in Guizhou (the poorest province in southwest China) (figure 2.7). In large classes, it is not possible to

Figure 2.6   Budgetary Revenues and Expenditures of the Subnational Government in China, 1990–2010

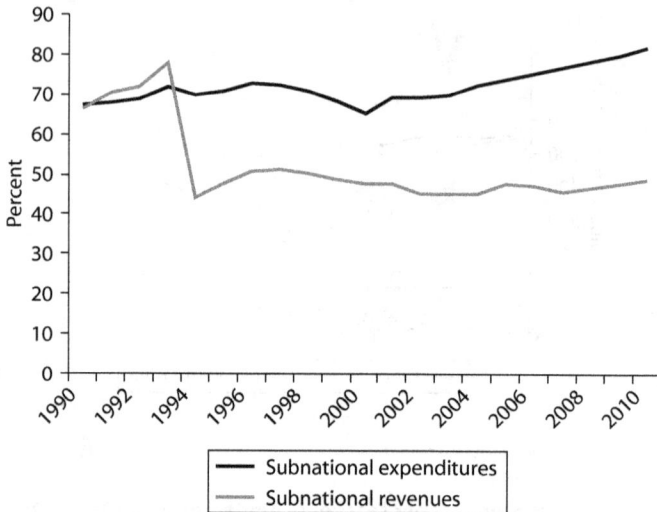

Source: NBS various years.

have a child-centered approach, and insufficient individual attention is paid to the development of language and cognitive skills. Large class size is less of a problem in the upper grades in compulsory education than in kindergartens because older students are developmentally more mature and capable of handling more abstract concepts, whereas young children need experiential approaches.

The distribution of teachers with specialized teacher qualifications reflects the unevenness in quality. In 2010, 40 percent of teachers with specialized teacher qualifications served in cities, 35 percent in county towns, and 24 percent in rural areas (figure 2.8). In rural areas, where more than 60 percent of children reside, there are fewer teachers with specialized qualifications to teach them.

Another indicator of quality is the percentage of substitute teachers (figure 2.9). The national average for public kindergartens was 6.5 percent. In rural schools, substitute teachers accounted for 13 percent of all teachers, compared with just 3 percent in cities and 7 percent in towns.

Substitute teachers in public kindergartens are less qualified than regular teachers. Information on private kindergartens and nurseries is not available. Given that 68 percent of kindergartens are private (accounting for 47 percent of the total enrollment in preprimary education in 2010),

Figure 2.7   Number of Students per Teacher in Kindergartens, by Province, 2010

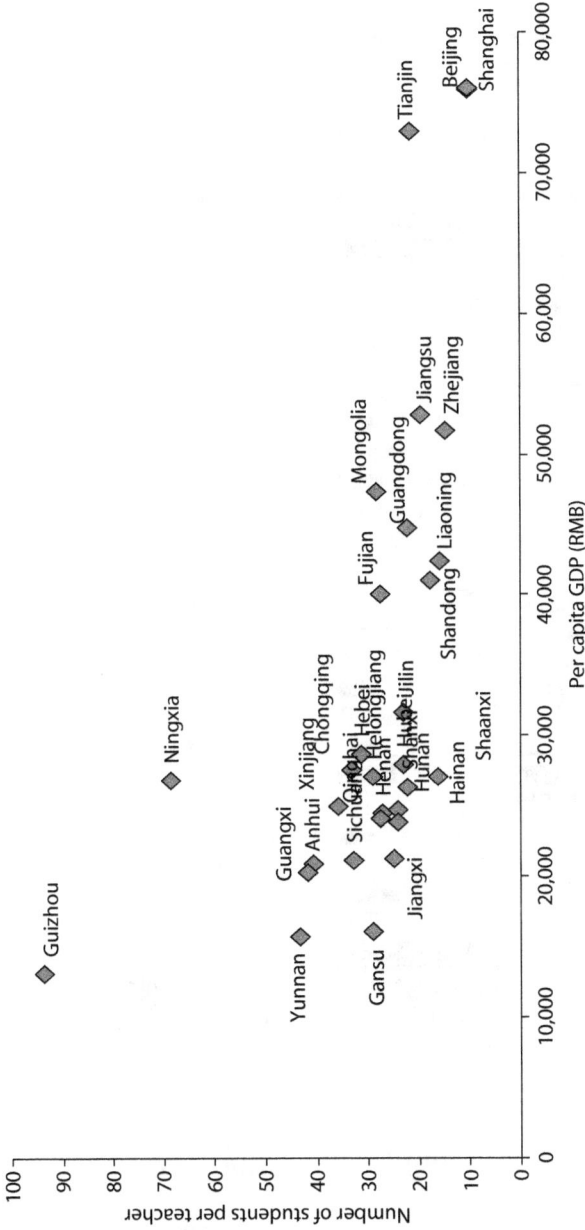

Source: MOE 2011.

Note: Tibet is an outlier and omitted from the graph. Figures include public and private kindergartens.

Figure 2.8   Percentage of Teachers in Kindergartens with Specialized Training, by Province, 2010

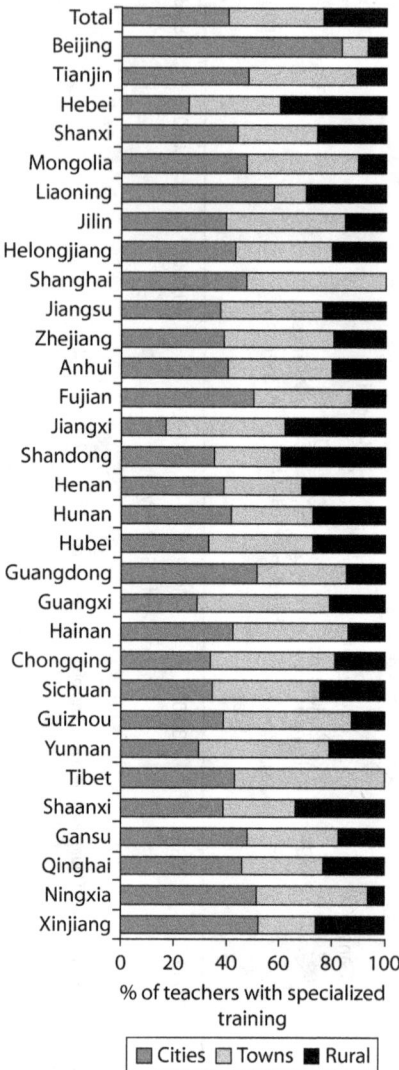

% of teachers with specialized training

■ Cities ☐ Towns ■ Rural

Source: MOE 2011.
Note: Figures include public and private kindergartens.

Figure 2.9   Substitute Teachers as Percentage of Total Kindergarten Teachers, 2010

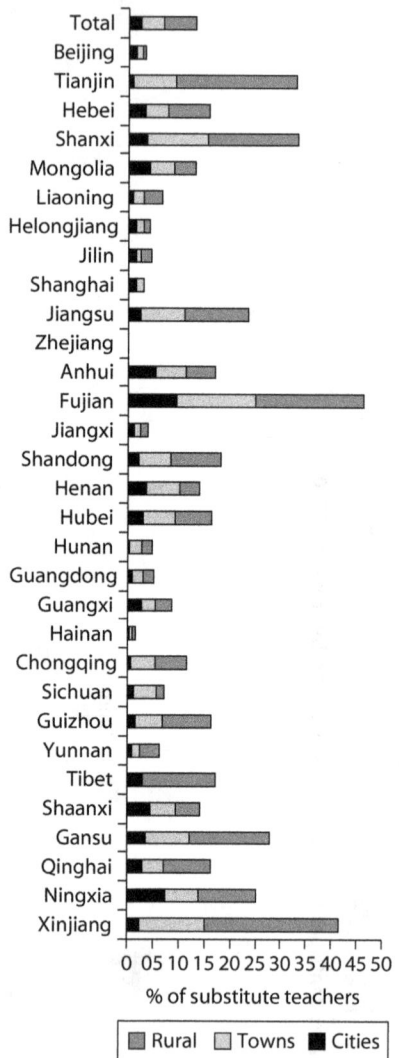

% of substitute teachers

■ Rural ☐ Towns ■ Cities

Source: MOE 2011.
Note: Figures include public and private kindergartens.

it would make sense to collect data on private kindergartens in order to inform policy.

All ECD teachers must be certified. Their ability to speak Mandarin must meet the minimum standard of attaining a B grade, and they must pass the examination on child psychology and education. The content of training comes from education theory (particularly the Montessori school of thought), psychology, public health, and medical information. Informal training offered to caregivers of children ages 0–6 is often conducted in workshops and seminars. It is also offered to parents. Government agencies such as the National Population and Family Planning Commission, the Ministry of Health, the Ministry of Education, the Ministry of Civil Affairs, and the Women's Federation conduct seminars in a variety of settings. Some preschools also invite child psychologists, early childhood educators, and pediatricians to give talks to parents.

Training and qualification of caregivers of children ages 0–3. The occupation standards of the Ministry of Human Resources and Labor Security govern the training content and qualification of caregivers of children ages 0–3. Training is conducted in vocational senior-secondary schools.

There are three levels for caregivers of infants and toddlers: caregiver, master, and senior master. Caregivers are required to complete junior-secondary education and take at least 80 standard learning hours of course work. Master caregivers are required to have five years of relevant working experience and at least 100 hours of course work. Senior master caregivers are required to have seven years of relevant experience and at least 120 hours of course work.

A key selection criteria for teachers of early child care and education programs is a personality with compassion and respect for children and the ability to learn. Basic knowledge covered includes physiology, psychology, and the nutritional and educational needs of children ages 0–3, as well as relevant laws. Caregivers are trained to handle real-life situations, such as feeding, creating comfortable environments for sleeping, bathing, changing diapers and clothing, ensuring hygienic conditions of the living environment, and sanitizing toys and food utensils. They are trained to monitor growth, follow the immunization schedule, prevent illness, deal with common childhood illness and injuries, and recognize the symptoms of lead poisoning. They are taught to help infants and toddlers develop gross and fine motor skills, acquire language, build good social skills and character, and master simple cognitive and math skills. Caregivers should be able to individualize instruction, assess infants' developmental progress, and guide the training of infants in developing skills.

Experts and service providers tend to focus on the care and education provided by professional caregivers. But the vast majority of young children are living at home, where they are cared for by parents or grandparents. Creating a new cadre of professionals who educate parents and primary caregivers at home would therefore be very beneficial.

Education and qualification of teachers and teaching assistants of children ages 3–6. Teaching assistants in kindergartens, social welfare institutes, and nurseries provide care to children and support teachers. There are three levels: elementary, middle, and senior. Teaching assistants at the elementary level have completed 120 hours of training. Teaching assistants at the middle level have had five years of experience and completed 140 hours of training. Teaching assistants at the senior level have had five years of experience after completing their middle-level training and completed 160 hours of training.

Assistants at the elementary level are required to have basic knowledge of physiology, health and hygiene, psychology, education, common childhood diseases, infectious diseases, first aid for common accidents and injuries, nutrition, and relevant laws. They must be able to sanitize the environment; provide three meals a day; bathe, toilet-train, and get children to sleep; follow the immunization schedule; ensure safety, prevent injury, and educate children about safety; and support the teacher in all indoor and outdoor activities.

Kindergarten teachers are prepared in vocational high schools, specialized secondary schools (normal schools at the senior-secondary level), three-year tertiary education institutions, and universities. They follow the curriculum set by the Ministry of Education.

There are two channels to becoming a teacher or teaching assistant. The first is to go through a senior-secondary level normal school with a specialization in early childhood education, a tertiary-level normal institution, or a normal university. The curriculum includes three theory courses (on early childhood education theory, child psychology, and child health) and six teaching method courses (on language, common knowledge, math, music, arts and crafts, and physical education). Students specializing in ECD must learn to draw, dance, and play a musical instrument in order to qualify as a teacher. They also have to complete a six-week practicum in a preschool. The entire training takes about three to four years. Upon graduation, students obtain certification as an early childhood teacher.

Students who were not educated in normal schools but are graduates of senior-secondary schools can take part in training for ECD to obtain qualification and the certification to teach. They have to take an examination in early childhood education, child psychology, Mandarin, and teaching of young children.

Since implementation of the Law on Teachers in 1993, ECD graduates can apply for a teaching certificate. In 2003, the State Council issued the *Guidelines Governing the Reform and Development of Early Childhood Education*, which clearly define in-service training of ECD teachers and treat them as part of professional development.

Linking preservice and in-service training. Although there has been progressive improvement in raising the standards of ECD teachers, the coordination of preservice and in-service training has yet to be established. Many policy makers believe that applying the preservice curriculum to in-service training will be adequate for teacher professional development. But teachers often encounter cases they were not taught in school. An example is autistic children, who respond to their peers far better than to adults. Mainstreaming and early intervention of autistic children can mitigate the severity of the disease. Preservice training separates special education and ECD, however, so that ECD teachers are not aware of the symptoms of autism or the techniques appropriate to working with autistic children. Onsite training and networking of teachers to deal with autistic children is now being conducted in a few schools in Shanghai.

Future preservice and in-service education and training could be more inclusive in terms of emerging problems, in order to address the issues facing children at risk more effectively. Issues could include psychological and safety problems of children left behind by their parents and the psychology, nutritional status, and safety of girls.

Notes

1. For an explanation of the various institutions that care for and educate children in China before they enter primary school, see box 1.1 in chapter 1 of this volume.

2. The targets are as follows: gross enrollment ratio (GER) for children starting kindergarten three years before grade 1 to increase from 51 percent in 2009 to 60 percent in 2015, GER for children starting kindergarten two years before grade 1 to increase from 65 percent to 70 percent, and GER

for children entering kindergarten one year before grade 1 to increase from 74 percent to 85 percent (see annex table 5A.2 for the targets). The GER targets for 2020 are 70 percent for children starting kindergarten three years before grade 1, 80 percent for children starting kindergarten two years before grade 1, and 95 percent for children starting kindergarten one year before grade 1 (see annex table 5A.2).

References

All-China Women's Federation, the National Population and Family Planning Commission, the Ministry of Education, the Ministry of Civil Affairs, the Ministry of Health, the Civilization Office of the Central Communist Party Committee, and the China National Committee for the Well-being of Youth. 2010. *National Guidelines on Family Education.* Beijing. (中华全国妇女联合会、国家人口和计划生育委员会、教育部、民政部、卫生部、中央文明办、中国关心下一代工作委员会。全国家庭教育指导大纲).

Corter, C., Z. Janmohammed, J. Zhang, and J. Bertland. 2006. "Selected Issues Concerning Early Childhood Care and Education in China." Background paper for *Education for All Global Monitoring Report 2007: Strong Foundations: Early Childhood Care and Education.* Paris: United Nations Education, Scientific and Cultural Organization (UNESCO).

Dai, Y. H. 2009. "Health and Safety of Children in China." Background paper commissioned by the World Bank for this book. East Asia Human Development Department. World Bank, Washington, DC. (中国儿童早期发展和教育的卫生与安全的现状与规范).

MOE (Ministry of Education). Various years: 2009, 2010, 2011a. *Educational Statistics Yearbook of China.* Department of Development and Planning. Beijing: People's Education Press. (教育部发展计划司。中国教育统计年鉴。不同年份。中国教育出版社。北京).

_____. 2011b. *National Plan for Improvement of Nutrition for Rural Students in Compulsory Education.* http://www.moe.edu.cn/publicfiles/business/htmfiles/moe/s6329/list.htm (全国农村义务教育学生营养改善计划).

NBS (National Bureau of Statistics of China). Various years. *China Statistical Yearbook.* Beijing: China Statistics Press. (国家统计局。中国统计年鉴。中国统计出版社。北京).

NPC (National People's Congress) and CPPCC (Chinese People's Political Consultative Conference). 2011. *Outline of the Twelfth Five Year Plan of National Economic and Social Development of China.* Beijing. http://www.gov.cn/2011h/content_1825838.htm (全国人民代表大会和中国人民政治协商会议。中国国民经济和社会发展第十二个五年规划纲要).

State Council. 2010a. *China's National Plan Outline for Medium- and Long-Term Education Reform and Development 2010–2020*. Beijing: State Council. http://www.gov.cn/jizg/2010-07/29. (国务院。国家中长期教育改革和发展规划纲要).

———. 2010b. *Guidelines on the Development of Pre-primary Education*. No. 41. 2010. Beijing State Council. http://www.gov.cn. (国务院关于当前发展学前教育的若干意见).

———. 2011a. *Development of the Elderly in the 12th Five-Year Plan*. Number 28. Beijing: State Council. http://www.gov.cn/zwgk/2011-09/23. (国务院。中国老龄事业发展"十二五"规划)

———. 2011b. *Guidelines on Chinese Women Development (2011–2020)* and *Guidelines on Chinese Children Development (2011–2020)*. No. 24. Beijing: State Council. http://www.gov.cn/2011-08/08. (国务院。中国妇女发展纲要 (2011–2020), 中国儿童发展纲要 (2011–2020).

———. 2011c. *Guidelines on Poverty Reduction and Development of Chinese Rural Areas (2011–2020)*. Beijing: State Council. http://www.gov.cn/jrzg/2011-12/01. (国务院。中国农村扶贫开发纲要).

———. 2011d. *Plan for Population Development in the 12th Five-Year Plan*. No. 39, 2011. Beijing: State Council. http://www.gov.cn/zwgk/2012-04/10. (国务院。国家人口发展十二五规划).

———. 2011e. *State Council Standing Committee Meeting Decision on Increase of Public Investment on the Development of Preprimary Education*. http://www.gov.cn/ldhd/2011-08/31/content_1937355.htm (国务院常务会议，决定增加财政投入支持发展学前教育)

UNICEF (United Nations Children's Fund). 2007. "ECD/ECCE in China." Presentation at UNESCO–UNICEF Joint Regional Workshop on Early Childhood Policy Review, Bangkok, February 6–8. http://www.unicef.org/eapro/China_Presentation.pdf.

Zhou, N. L. 2010. "Report on Preservice Training of Teachers of 0–3 Age Groups and 3–6 Age Groups, Regulation on kindergartens, and Facility Standards." Draft. Prepared as a background note for the World Bank. (0-3岁的早教培训, 3-6岁教师的职前培训, 幼儿园工作规程, 幼儿园建筑设计规范).

CHAPTER 3

Financing Early Child Development

The disparity in access to service has its roots in China's decentralized system of finance. Although China is highly centralized in terms of policy and regulation, it is highly decentralized in finance and administration. Current expenditure assignments place the heaviest financial burdens on the lowest levels of government—county governments in rural areas and district governments in municipalities. In 2008, governments at the county and township levels accounted for 45 percent of total budgetary spending on education, compared with 10 percent for the central government and 45 percent for provinces (World Bank 2009a).

The central government places emphasis on providing nine years of free compulsory education, for good reasons. The rural compulsory education finance reform during the 11th Five-Year Plan (2006–2010) exempted miscellaneous fees for all rural students, gradually eliminated textbook fees for all students, and provided targeted boarding subsidies to poor students. To compensate for the elimination of fees, central fiscal transfers cover 80 percent of the cost in 12 provinces in the Western region and 60 percent in 10 provinces in the Central region. The richer coastal provinces and urban areas are required to use their own resources to finance free compulsory education. In 2008, miscellaneous fees and textbook fees were abolished nationwide (World Bank 2009b).

The substantial increase in budgetary expenditure per student in compulsory education was made possible not only by China's growing wealth but also by the declining size of the school-age population (figure 3.1). Intrasectoral budgetary allocation remained stable over time (figure 3.2). Although enrollment in preschool is higher than it was in the 1980s, the share of budgetary expenditure has hardly changed. The budgetary allocation to preprimary education is so small that it is barely visible in figure 3.2.

Because local governments lack the fiscal capacity to fund them, nurseries and kindergartens rely heavily on fees for financing. Even public sector institutions are fee based.[1] Some local governments with stronger finances give priority to support for industry and to investments that build the local image. Much less attention has been paid to investments in human development, the economic returns from which, although high, have a much longer time horizon.

The private sector plays an active role in the provision of services to children ages 0–6. In 2010, 68 percent of nurseries and kindergartens were private, accounting for 47 percent of enrollment. By contrast, private institutions accounted for just 5 percent of primary enrollment, 14 percent of

Figure 3.1   Distribution of Students in China, by Level of Education, 1980–2010

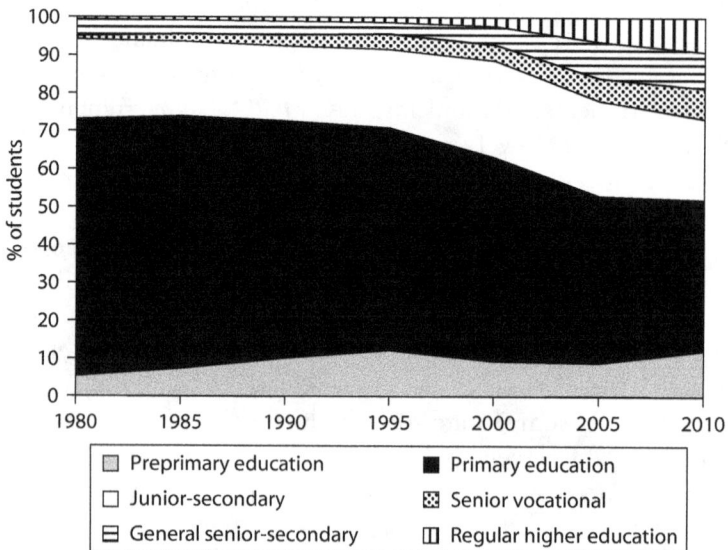

Legend:
- ▨ Preprimary education
- ■ Primary education
- ☐ Junior-secondary
- ▨ Senior vocational
- ⊟ General senior-secondary
- ⊞ Regular higher education

Source: MOE various years.
Note: Because of the relatively small number of students in special education, and the small amount of the budget allocated to it, special education does not show up in the graph but it is recorded in the official statistics.

Figure 3.2   Budgetary Expenditure on Education in China, by Level of Education, 1995–2010

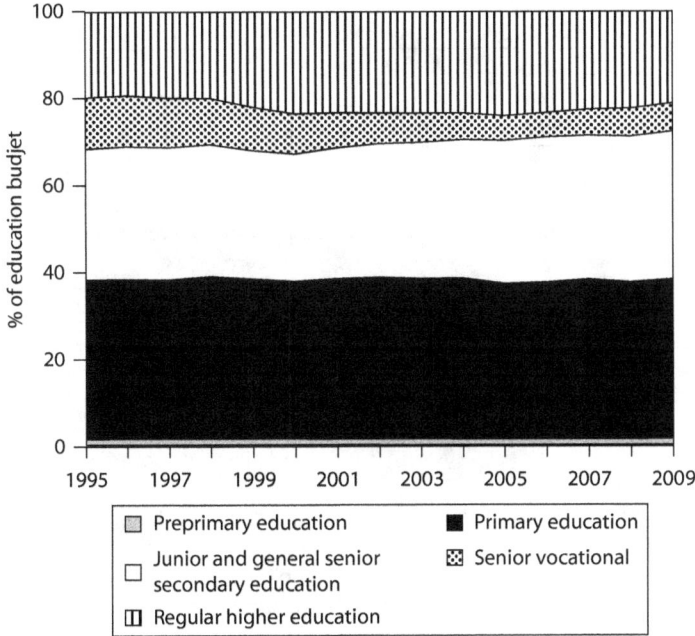

Source: MOE and NBS various years.
Note: Because of the relatively small number of students in special education, and the small amount of the budget allocated to it, special education does not show up in the graph but it is recorded in the official statistics.

enrollment in technical and vocational education at the senior-secondary level, and 12 percent of enrollment in higher education (MOE 2011).

Because public kindergartens are larger than private kindergartens, they represented 32 percent of all kindergartens in China but they accounted for 53 percent of enrollment. Table 3.1 shows the number of public and private kindergartens and enrollment in each sector.

Household spending is the main source of financing of kindergartens, in both the public and private sectors. As such, inability to pay is a key barrier to access. Table 3.2 presents the sources of funds of different types of early child development services.

Public Expenditure on Preprimary Education

China's budgetary spending on education represented 3.5 percent of gross domestic product (GDP) in 2009, an increase from the historical trend of less than 3 percent throughout most of the 1980s to 2007. Given China's double-digit economic growth rate over the past two decades and

Table 3.1   Number of and Enrollment in Public and Private Kindergartens in China, 2010

Sector	Number of kindergartens (thousands)	Percent	Enrollment (thousands)	Percent
Public	48.1	32	15,772	53
Private	102.3	68	13,995	47
Total	150.4	100	29,767	100

Source: MOE 2011.

Table 3.2   Main Public Sources of Funding of Early Child Development Programs in China

Type of institution	Main sources of funding
Informal care and education institutions	• Donations from nonstate sectors and other funds raised by institutions • Fees
Formal kindergartens and preprimary classes (for children 3–6) Public institutions Institutions affiliated with enterprises, institutions, governmental bodies, and so forth Institutions run by urban neighborhoods and collective units Institutions run by rural neighborhoods and collective units	• Budgetary appropriations by enterprises, institutions, and governmental bodies • Fees • Subsidies for capital costs • Local (township or village) governments • Public dues • Donations

Source: UNESCO 2003.

the increase in government revenue, this amount represents an increase in real terms in the aggregate and on a per student basis for all subsectors of education. This level of public spending is still below the 4 percent of GDP called for by the country's own Education Law, however, and it is much lower than the average of 5.9 percent spent in Organisation for Economic Co-operation and Development (OECD) countries in 2008 (OECD 2011).[2]

To guarantee that the increase in the allocation to education exceeds the increase in revenue, *China's National Plan Outline for Medium- and Long-Term Education Reform and Development 2010–2020* states that public expenditure on education will be given priority and protected in the budget process. Specifically, 3 percent of the value added, business, and consumption taxes will contribute to an educational fund used only for education purposes. The target is to increase public spending on education to 4 percent of GDP by 2012.

Total education expenditures include both budgetary allocation of government expenditures and the extrabudgetary funds shown in table 3.2. The sources of extrabudgetary funds are similar at all levels of education. These extrabudgetary funds are for public institutions only. Private institutions are completely dependent on fees, which are not accounted for in official statistics.

The intrasectoral allocation of budgetary expenditure does not reflect the share of student enrollment in the public education system as a whole. In 2009, higher education accounted for 12 percent of total enrollment in public institutions but received 20 percent of the budget. This share is slightly lower than the OECD average of 25 percent (OECD 2011). Budgetary expenditure on junior-secondary education was roughly proportional to its share of enrollment in public institutions; budgetary spending on primary education was below its share of total enrollment in the public sector.

Preprimary education has been the most seriously underfunded subsector. In 2009, this subsector accounted for 7 percent of enrollment in public institutions but received only 1 percent of the education budget (table 3.3). In 2009, extrabudgetary spending in preprimary education (most of it tuition fees) accounted for 38 percent of total spending. By comparison, extrabudgetary spending accounted for 11 percent of spending on primary education, 15 percent on junior-secondary education, 26 percent on senior-secondary education, 41 percent on technical and vocational education and training (TVET), and 53 percent on tertiary education.

China's budgetary spending on preprimary education was about 0.1 percent of GDP in 2008—much lower than the OECD average public spending on preprimary education of 0.4 percent of GDP (OECD 2011). Iceland was the highest-spending country in 2008, devoting 1.0 percent of its GDP to preprimary education; Israel and Spain spent about 0.8 percent; and Denmark, Sweden, Hungary, Mexico, France, the Russian Federation, and Chile spent 0.6–0.7 percent (figure 3.3).

China's public expenditure on preprimary education is so low because responsibility for financing and provision of service rests with the lowest level of government—county governments in rural areas and district governments in urban areas. The lack of fiscal capacity of these levels of governments has constrained the supply of early child development (ECD) services, including preprimary education. Although there is a similar financing arrangement for compulsory education (primary and junior-secondary education), the central government provides fiscal transfers to poor provinces and counties to make up for their shortfalls in

Table 3.3 Enrollment in and Budgetary Shares Allocated to Public Institutions in China, by Level of Education, 2009

percent, except where otherwise indicated

Level of education	Enrollment	Public budgetary spending	Extrabudgetary funds as share of total spending	Level of government responsible for financing and providing service
Higher education	12	20	53	Ministry of Education, provinces, autonomous regions, municipalities
General senior-secondary	9	9	26	Provinces, autonomous regions, municipalities
Technical and vocational	8	6	41	Provinces, autonomous regions, municipalities
Junior-secondary	21	22	15	Counties, districts
Primary	42	33	11	Counties, districts
Kindergartens and preprimary schools	7	1	38	Counties, districts
Special education	0.2	0.4	16	Counties, districts
Other, including administration	0.3	8	27	
Total				
Percent (rounded)	100	100	31	
Numbers	233 million students	RMB1,142 billion ($168 billion)		

Sources: MOE and NBS 2010; MOE 2011.

Figure 3.3   Public Spending on Preprimary Education for Children Age 3 and Older as a Percentage of GDP in Selected Countries, 2008

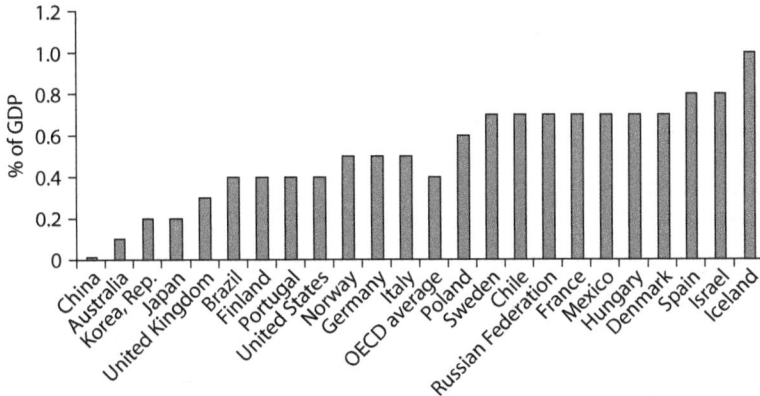

Sources: OECD 2011; MOE and NBS 2010.

resources in order to enable them to provide free compulsory education. In contrast, central fiscal transfers are not available to preprimary education, because it is not compulsory. At the postcompulsory level (senior-secondary education, TVET, and higher education), responsibility for financing and providing service rests with provincial or municipal governments. These higher levels of government are in a better financial position to fund their mandates.

Cost recovery has played a key role in financing preprimary and post-compulsory education. The effect of cost-recovery for post-compulsory education is mitigated by the availability of annual stipends to all TVET students and general senior-secondary education students who are poor and by grants and loans for tertiary education[3]. In contrast, neither grants nor loans are available to support ECD services for the poor and vulnerable.

Per student spending on preprimary education in China is high compared with spending on primary education. Budgetary spending on pre-primary per student is 1.1 times that of primary education; when extrabudgetary spending is included, it is 1.5 times higher (table 3.4). By comparison, in OECD countries and Brazil, per student public spending on preprimary education is lower than public spending on primary education. Only Chile allocates a larger share than China. The high average cost of preprimary education in China makes it difficult for local governments to finance its expansion.

Table 3.4   Public Spending per Student on Various Levels of Education in Selected Countries
primary education = 1.0

Country	Preprimary	Junior-secondary	Senior-secondary	Tertiary
China (2008)				
Budgetary	1.1	1.2	1.4	3.6
Budgetary and extrabudgetary (fees and donations)	1.5	1.3	1.3	6.9
OECD average (2005)	0.8	1.2	1.3	1.8
Japan	0.6	1.1	1.2	1.8
Korea, Rep.	0.5	1.2	1.7	1.6
United States	0.9	1.1	1.2	2.7
Brazil (2005)	0.9	1.7	0.6	7.0
Chile (2005)	1.5	1.0	1.0	3.4

Sources: MOE and NBS 2008; OECD 2008.

In all subsectors, the range of per student public spending across and within provinces is wide. Figure 3.4 plots provincial per capita GDP against provincial budgetary expenditure, as well as total expenditure by provinces (which includes both budgetary and extrabudgetary spending) (also see annex table 3A.1). Extrabudgetary expenditure comes from tuition, own-generated income, and donations. Fees account for the bulk of extrabudgetary expenditures on preprimary education.

Both budgetary and total expenditure show wide divergence between the poorer and rich provinces and municipalities. Shanghai had the highest per capita GDP in the country (RMB78,989 [$11,616]) in 2009 and also the highest budgetary spending per student on preprimary education (RMB10,246 [$1,506]). It spent 17 times more on preprimary education than Guangxi (RMB600 [$88]). Its per student budgetary expenditure on preprimary education is higher than per student budgetary expenditure on tertiary education in many provinces.[4]

Given the significant impact of preprimary education on poverty alleviation and improvement of school readiness, underfunding of this subsector is likely to exact a high social cost.

The divergence in spending per student by province also captures disparities in quality. Preprimary education has the widest gap in budgetary and extrabudgetary spending per student between the top-spending municipalities and the lowest-spending provinces. Ironically, wealthier provinces (for example, Zhejiang) have lower budgetary allocations, because parents there are more willing and able to pay out of pocket.

In industrial countries, the extent of state support for preprimary education tends to be related to the labor force participation of women and

Figure 3.4   Budgetary and Total Spending per Student on Preprimary Education in China, by Province, 2009

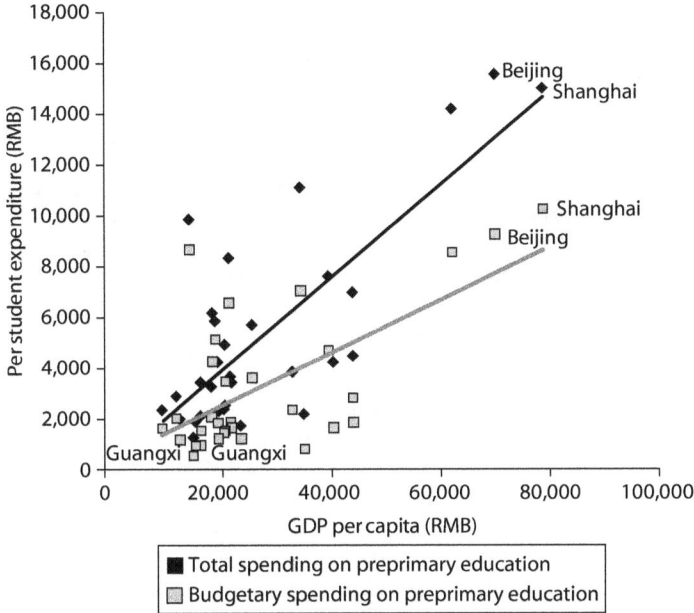

societal attitudes toward the family. The Nordic countries provide high levels of family welfare and child care, facilitating women's participation in the labor force (table 3.5). English-speaking countries (Australia and New Zealand, Canada, the United States, and the United Kingdom) rely on the family and the market to meet the need for child care, resulting in lower female participation in the labor force than in northern Europe. In Western Europe, family welfare is high but female participation relatively low because of societal attitudes that value women taking care of their own children. Yet attendance in kindergarten is very high. Japan and countries in Southern European rely on the market and families to provide child care. China has a relatively high rate of female participation in the labor force (62 percent in urban areas and 79 percent in rural areas), about the same as English-speaking countries.

Private Finance and Provision of Preprimary Education and Childcare Services

Before the reform of 1978, all kindergartens and childcare facilities were in the public sector, run by ministries, state-owned enterprises, or collectives.

Table 3.5   Labor Force Participation by Women and Child Care Policy in Selected Countries

Level of labor force participation by women	Child care and family welfare	Countries
Very high	State provides high level of family welfare and childcare.	Denmark, Finland, Norway, Sweden
Relatively high	Family and the market bear responsibility for child care. There is no comprehensive family welfare policy.	Australia, Canada, China, New Zealand, United Kingdom, United States
Relatively low	Women are expected to take care of their own children, but level of family welfare is high.	Austria, Belgium, France, Germany, Netherlands
Low	Responsibility for child care rests with family and the market.	Iceland, Ireland, Italy, Japan Portugal, Spain, Switzerland

Source: Liu and Dong 2008.

After the transition to a market economy, these public sector agencies separated welfare services such as kindergartens from their core business in order to cut costs. Some kindergartens became private, run by the retrenched staff. Over time, an increasing number of kindergartens, particularly in cities and towns, were established by private individuals or groups and run like businesses.

Given China's family planning policy, families tend to spare no efforts to provide for their children. This thinking has largely fueled the development of the market for private kindergartens. Figure 3.5 shows that whereas no private kindergartens were in existence in 1986, 68 percent of kindergartens were private by 2010.

As preprimary education is financed by user charges, inability to pay is a barrier to access. Private expenditure accounts for an estimated 70 percent of total expenditure on preprimary education in China, when user fees in both public and private institutions are included. The OECD average was 18.5 percent in 2008 (figure 3.6). Private spending in China dwarfed private spending even in Australia, Japan, and the Republic of Korea, where private resources accounted for than 50 percent of total spending on preprimary education.

Fees charged for kindergartens vary widely. Private kindergartens are free to set their own fees, but they need to report them to the local government (approval is pro forma). Their rates are market based. On the whole, public kindergartens have lower totally monthly fees but higher

Figure 3.5   Ownership of and Enrollment in Private and Public Kindergartens in China, 1986–2008

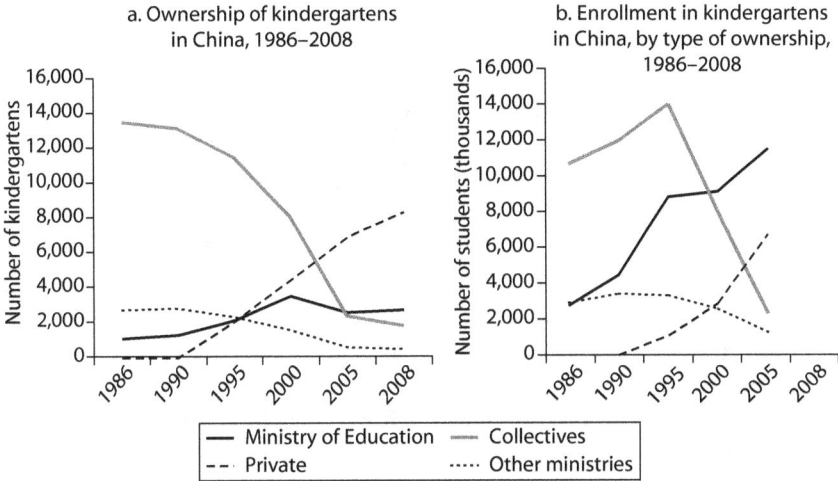

a. Ownership of kindergartens in China, 1986–2008

b. Enrollment in kindergartens in China, by type of ownership, 1986–2008

— Ministry of Education   — Collectives
-- Private   ..... Other ministries

Source: MOE various years.

Figure 3.6   Private Expenditure as a Percentage of Total Expenditure on Preprimary Education Institutions in Selected Countries, 2008

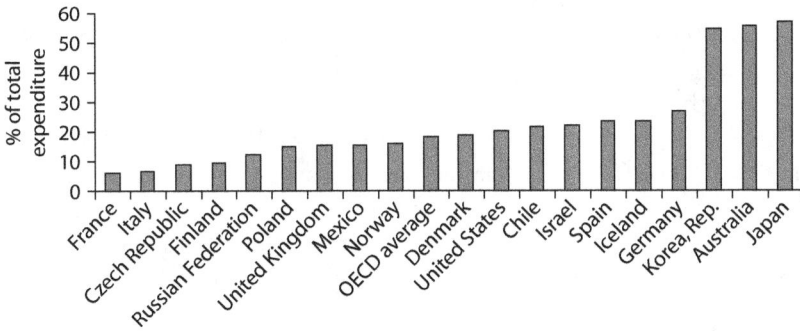

Source: OECD 2011.

"sponsorship fees," usually one-time payments made in order to gain admission. Sponsorship fees contribute to the capital of kindergartens. They are used to renovate classrooms; buy equipment (HDTVs, computers, DVDs, musical instruments); undertake repairs and maintenance; and beautify the premises. These fees can be hefty.

Monthly fees cover the cost of teaching and learning materials (mostly consumables, such as papers for drawing) and food. Government subsidies usually cover the salaries of teachers and staff and provisions for the premises. Public kindergartens usually receive free land and buildings; private kindergartens have to purchase land or rent their premises. Public kindergartens tend to be of higher quality than private kindergartens, with more space and better qualified teachers. Demand for them is also higher, allowing them to charge higher sponsorship fees (see annex tables 3A.2–3A.4 for the tuition fees charged in kindergartens in Shaanxi and Guangdong provinces and other selected provinces).

Fees can be classified into three categories:

- The most expensive kindergartens cost in 2008 about RMB30,000–RMB50,000 ($4,411–$7,353) a year, inclusive of sponsorship fees, management fees, food, insurance, uniforms, books, notebooks, computers, utilities (air conditioning), and activities. The higher end of the fee structure includes boarding. These facilities tend to be Chinese-English bilingual and include a health room, a dance room, a game room, and a drawing room. Teachers are highly qualified.
- A medium-range kindergarten costs about RMB800–RMB3,000 ($118–$441) a year, exclusive of sponsorship fees. The fees cover learning materials, but the facilities are not as well equipped as higher-end facilities.
- Very small-scale private kindergartens, which charge RMB130–RMB800 ($19–$118) a year, excluding sponsorship fees and boarding.

To put these fee levels in perspective, in 2009 average rural income in China was RMB 5,135 ($755), and some 36 million people lived on less than RMB1,196 ($176) a year. Inability to pay is thus the main barrier to access on the demand side, with the scarcity of kindergartens the main barrier to access on the supply side. Without intervention, preprimary education could become education for the elite.

Cost Drivers

Both supply and demand factors explain why preprimary education costs as much as if not more than primary education. On the supply side, high-quality kindergarten is child and activity centered; it requires low student-to-teacher and student-to-staff ratios. The activities and length of the school day are also very different from compulsory education, requiring much more space and intensive supervision of children.

The government provides guidelines on the number, types, and sizes of rooms at kindergartens (see annex table 3A.5). Given the high cost of real estate, particularly in Chinese cities, the space requirements drive up costs, which in turn drive up fees.

On the demand side, the fact that families in China have just one child means that parents who can afford to are willing to pay dearly to give their only child a head start. However, high fees are a barrier to access for the poor.

Services for Children, Ages 0–3

There is no standard curriculum or centrally issued guideline for service provision. Instead, every provider defines its own offering, drawn from the theory of child development. Generally, parent-teacher classes and nurseries aim to stimulate babies to crawl and eventually walk and to develop their sensory motor skills, language skills, confidence, and curiosity. Box 3.1 describes some of the activities in parent-child classes. The labor-intensity of this kind of service makes it expensive to provide.

Box 3.1

The National Population and Family Planning Commission's Early Child Development Centers

In a country that has only 7 percent of the world's land (of which less than half is arable) but 20 percent of the world's population, the National Population and Family Planning Commission's (NPFPC) has played a key role in stabilizing the population to ensure the people can meet their basic needs for food and clothing and facilitating a more harmonious relationship between economic development, resources, and the environment. The NPFPC aims to implement long-term measures to raise the capability of the population. For this reason, it gives top priority to raising the overall quality of human development, emphasizing ECD to give children a head start.

NPFPC provides a range of services, including counseling on family planning and provision of contraceptives; prenatal and postnatal, family-based, and elder care; and immunization and early child development services. It also provides exercise classes for pregnant women; early stimulation classes for infants, toddlers, and their mothers; and outreach to rural areas to advise on parenting skills and child growth monitoring.

With instruction and supervision from NPFPC, some 50 demonstration early development centers have been established nationwide. These centers provide

(continued next page)

Box 3.1 *(continued)*

the venue for children without siblings to interact with other children and for parents to exchange experiences. The centers provide prenatal classes, baby swimming lessons (in a bath tub), and parent-child (*Qinzi*) classes, all of which are grouped by age clusters of 9–15, 16–22, 23–29, and 30–36 months. NPFPC also operates regular nurseries. Services are based on fees or monthly subscriptions.

Parent-child classes may have 10 or more children and their parents/ grandparents or nannies. They include organized activities such as play, song and dance, and exercises designed to develop motor skills. A qualified instructor provides guidance in these structured activities. *Qinzi* classes are organized during the day and evening, usually on weekends. Fees are charged on an hourly basis, ranging from RMB50 to RMB120 ($7.40–$17.60) per hour. Fees for nurseries are on a monthly basis.

The early development center in the Qinghe County of Hebei Province has about 160 children ages 2–6. Another 600 children attend classes or sessions offered by the center, and about 80 children are on the waiting list. The facility is well equipped and staffed. The head of the program is well versed in early child care and development and trained in maternal and child health. The center also offers an outreach program to train village staff on home visits within the county. It has also developed and published a set of ECD materials, which are distributed countywide.

Source: World Bank mission visit, July 2009.

Services for Children, Ages 3–6

Preprimary education aims to provide experiential learning, so that children achieve well-rounded development through various organized and guided activities that promote physical, cognitive, language, emotional, social, and fine and gross motor development.

The aim of preprimary education is comprehensive and developmental. Its content needs to be rooted in life, so that children can relate to it, and integrative, with subjects relating to one another other. Children can engage in activities independently, with a partner, or in a group. Activities take place indoors or outdoors. Toys are used to stimulate imagination and curiosity and help children learn different roles in society. The type and level of activities must be appropriate to the age of children. Development of more abstract concepts takes place at a later age.

The Ministry of Education's *Guidelines on Kindergarten Education* (2001) emphasizes the formation of good habits, initiative, curiosity, and eagerness to learn. The content of preprimary education is divided into health, language, social, science, and art domains. It requires the integration of attitudes, feelings, cognition, and skills. These guidelines led to major changes in ECD approaches. Thematic approaches (such as seasons and festivals) are adopted to teach related concepts, and different activities are organized to teach these themes. The activity-based approach gives kindergarten directors and teachers much discretion in determining offerings.

Kindergarten classes are supposed to ease children's transition to compulsory education, but there is a tendency to advance the curriculum for primary 1 to kindergarten, teaching math, language, reading, and writing, leaving too little time for play. Table 3.6 compares activities in kindergarten and primary school. Box 3.2 offers a glimpse into a day in the life of a kindergarten in Changchun city, in Jilin Province in Northeast China.

Children are prepared for primary education during the last year of preschool (preprimary) by focusing on completing a task within a given time frame, being self-directed, acquiring self-discipline, and being able to express their needs and questions orally. Preprimary school thus provides the transition to compulsory education.

Table 3.6   Instructional Time, Classroom Management, and Instructional Approaches in Kindergarten and Primary School in China

Feature	Kindergarten	Primary school
Duration of class	1–1.5 hours of collective instruction per day, 30 minutes per session. Rest of day includes games, playing, and physical activities.	4.0–4.5 hours a day of collective instruction per day, 40 minutes per session.
Classroom management	Activities change five times a day.	Strict enforcement of rules in class and clearly defined recess time.
Instructional approach	Centers on games and playing, development of fine and gross motor skills, cumulative experience, and knowledge by doing.	Follows centrally defined curriculum guidelines; teachers required to deliver curriculum, focus on learning process, and test learning outcomes.
Relationship between teachers and students	At least two adults (teacher and assistant) supervise a class; there is adult supervision every single minute.	Five to six teachers teach different subjects in a given grade. There is a turnaround of teachers at the end of a session, with no supervision between classes.
Content of instruction	Concrete, visual, lively transmission of knowledge.	Systematic knowledge and abstract concepts are taught. A single teacher uses traditional stand-and-deliver method to teach a large class.

Source: Liu 2009.

Box 3.2

A Day in the Life of a Kindergarten in Changchun, Jilin Province

The kindergarten visited has 26 children (5-year-olds), one teacher, and very few toys. Most of the children brought their own toys from home. Every child had a book bag, in which they put their books, clothing, food, and toys. In the afternoon, they napped on foldable beds in the classroom. The daily schedule is described below.

7:30–8:20	Arrival, breakfast.
8:20–8:50	Free activities.
8:50–9:20	Children were instructed on numbers. They add and subtract numbers lower than 10. Most children did not understand but recited the multiplication table.
9:20–9:30	Rest, drink water, go to bathroom, play.
9:30–10:00	Children were taught *pinying* (use of Latin alphabets to represent sounds in Chinese). Teacher required children to put their hands on the desk and not speak to one another or walk around. If students answered correctly, the teacher praised them. Children who did not pay attention were asked to stand aside as punishment.
10:00–10:10	Worksheet distributed that required parental signature. Homework takes about half an hour.
10:40–11:10	Hand washing in preparation for lunch.
11:20–11:50	Half of the class took art and dance lessons, at extra charge. These lessons took place twice a week. Other students took afternoon nap.
12:00–14:00	Afternoon nap.
14:00–14:30	Snack, fruit.
14:30–15:00	English class was held for two-thirds of students whose parents pay extra for it.
15:00	Sing songs, read books, and then watch TV while waiting for parents to pick them up.

Source: October 2005 observation (see Liu 2009).

The labor intensity of teaching and supervision and the need for space for a variety of activities contribute to the high cost of preprimary education. The high cost deters universalization of preprimary education. To make services accessible to the poor, policy makers should explore alternative lower-cost but high-quality modes of delivery.

Annex 3A Finance and Cost of Early Child Development

Table 3A.1   Budgetary and Total per Student Spending on Preprimary Education in China, by Province, 2009

Province	GDP per capita RMB	GDP per capita $	Total spending on preprimary education per student RMB	Total spending on preprimary education per student $	Budgetary spending on preprimary education per student RMB	Budgetary spending on preprimary education per student $
Shanghai	78,989	11,616	15,060	2,215	10,246	1,507
Beijing	70,452	10,361	15,607	2,295	9,254	1,361
Tianjin	62,574	9,202	14,238	2,094	8,554	1,258
Jiangsu	44,744	6,580	4,527	666	1,888	278
Zhejiang	44,641	6,565	7,014	1,031	2,857	420
Guangdong	41,166	6,054	4,281	630	1,673	246
Mongolia	40,282	5,924	7,642	1,124	4,722	694
Shandong	35,894	5,279	2,230	328	857	126
Liaoning	35,239	5,182	11,152	1,640	7,041	1,035
Fujian	33,840	4,976	3,885	571	2,377	350
Jilin	26,595	3,911	5,741	844	3,636	535
Hebei	24,581	3,615	1,778	261	1,255	185
Chongqing	22,920	3,371	3,473	511	1,677	247
Hubei	22,677	3,335	3,699	544	1,905	280
Helongjiang	22,447	3,301	8,362	1,230	6,572	967
Ningxia	21,777	3,203	2,574	379	1,563	230
Shaanxi	21,688	3,189	4,961	730	3,481	512
Shanxi	21,522	3,165	2,425	357	1,487	219
Henan	20,597	3,029	2,349	346	1,245	183
Hunan	20,428	3,004	4,281	630	1,868	275
Xinjiang	19,942	2,933	5,886	866	5,137	755
Qinghai	19,454	2,861	6,212	913	4,275	629
Hainan	19,254	2,831	3,313	487	2,110	310
Sichuan	17,339	2,550	2,155	317	993	146
Jiangxi	17,335	2,549	3,475	511	1,584	233
Anhui	16,408	2,413	1,932	284	966	142
Guangxi	16,045	2,360	1,309	192	600	88
Tibet	15,295	2,249	9,886	1,454	8,653	1,273
Yunnan	13,539	1,991	2,031	299	1,208	178
Gansu	12,872	1,893	2,927	430	2,028	298
Guizhou	10,309	1,516	2,389	351	1,667	245

Source: MOE and NBS 2010.

Table 3A.2   Monthly Fees Charged by Public Kindergartens in Shaanxi Province, 2008

RMB

Type of service	Standard rate
Provincial-level demonstration kindergarten	
Whole day	130
Boarding	180
Type 1 kindergarten	
Whole day	90
Boarding	130
Type 2 kindergarten	
Whole day	70
Boarding	100
Type 3 kindergarten	
Whole day	50
Boarding	75
Not yet classified	
Whole day	35
Boarding	55

Source: Shaanxi Price Bureau website, reported in Liu 2009
Note: Type indicates size and facilities.

Table 3A.3   Fees Charged by Public Kindergartens in Guangdong Province, 2008

Kindergarten	Type	Fee
Academy of Science Kindergarten	Provincial Type 1	RMB12,000/year, and one time sponsorship fee
Guangzhou Municipality Kindergarten	Provincial Type 1	RMB5,000/year
Guangzhou Municipality Number 1	Provincial Type 1	RMB10,000/year
Huanghua Road Kindergarten	Provincial Type 1	RMB15,000 for four years
Kindergarten attached to South China Agricultural University	Municipal Type 1	RMB3,000/year for children and grandchildren of employees; RMB5,000/year for outsiders
Kindergarten attached to South China Normal University	Provincial Type 1	RMB11,000/year for children and grandchildren of employees; RMB15,000/year for outsiders
Little North Road Air Force Logistic Kindergarten	Municipal Type 1	RMB5,000/year
Provincial Kindergarten Number 1	Provincial Type 1	RMB10,000/year
Provincial Kindergarten Number 2	Provincial Type 1	RMB12,000/year

Source: http://baby.sina.com.cn/news/2008-09-09/083734933.shtml 2009-06-22, reported in Liu 2009.

Table 3A.4 Fees Charged for One-Year Preprimary School in Selected Provinces of China, 2009

RMB

Province	Fees charged						Fee standard set by government			
	Public			Private			Public		Private	
	Average	Maximum	Minimum	Average	Maximum	Minimum	Maximum	Minimum	Maximum	Minimum
Guangxi										
City	2,120	3,500	740	7,050	13,600	500	4,000	740	13,600	500
Towns	1,313	2,400	225	2,350	4,500	200	2,400	225	4,800	200
Rural	853	1,600	105	1,045	1,890	200	1,600	105	3,000	200
Jiangsu										
City	1,520	2,087	800	2,978	5,332	864	2,061	849	5,651	999
Towns	1,180	1,723	686	1,387	2,284	701	1,783	706	2,378	780
Rural	880	1,327	427	969	1,613	569	1,503	477	2,165	634
Hubei										
City	1,115	2,050	180	4,660	9,000	320	2,050	320	6,250	320
Towns	780	1,300	260	1,600	3,000	200	1,300	300	3,000	200
Rural	415	680	150	350	550	150	2,050	150	1,020	120
Hebei										
City	855	1,600	110	3,445	6,800	90	1,600	110	6,000	90
Towns	505	970	40	2,065	4,080	50	950	40	4,080	50
Rural	290	540	40	1,075	2,100	50	950	40	1,500	50
Chongqing										
City	367	595	130	288	480	65	250	50	To follow Instruction from	
Towns	148	310	52	134	230	41	250	50	Ministry of Education	
Rural	89	161	32	107	250	41	250	50		
Liaoning										
City	220	980	40	427	2,000	40	550	40	2,350	
Towns	120	400	40	160	500	35	230	40	400	
Rural	83	350	25	121	360	40	200	30	200	

Source: Liu 2009.

Table 3A.5 Guidelines on Facilities in Urban Kindergartens

Room	Size (sq. meters)	Schools with 6 classrooms (180 students)		School with 9 classrooms (270 students)		School with 12 classrooms (360 students)	
		Number of rooms	Total space (sq. meters)	Number of rooms	Total space (sq. meters)	Number of rooms	Total space (sq. meters)
Activity and other rooms							
Activity rooms	90	6	540	9	810	12	1,080
Children's bathroom	15	6	90	9	135	12	180
Storage room for toys and materials	9	6	90	9	81	12	180
Music room	—	1	120	1	140	1	160
Subtotal	—	—	804	—	1,166	—	1,528
Square meters per student	—	—	4.47	—	4.32	—	4.24
Office and related rooms							
Office	—	—	75	—	112	—	139
Material and conference room	—	1	20	1	25	1	30
Room for materials and display	—	1	12	1	15	1	20
Health room	—	1	14	1	16	1	18
Morning inspection and reception room	—	1	18	1	21	1	24
Guards' room	12	1	12	1	12	1	12
Storage room	—	3	36	4	42	4	48
Visit announcement room	10	1	10	1	10	1	10
Staff bathroom	—	—	12	—	12	—	12
Subtotal	—	—	209	—	265	—	313

Square meters per student	—	1.16	0.98	0.87
Living rooms				
Kitchen	—	54	61	67
Food storage room	—	15	20	30
Furnace	—	8	9	10
Water boiler	—	8	10	12
Room for kitchen staff	—	13	18	23
Subtotal	—	98	118	142
Square meters per student	—	0.54	0.43	0.39
Total				
Floor area	—	1,111	1,549	1,983
Space per student	—	6.17	5.74	5.51

Source: Zhou 2010.
Note: — = not available.

Notes

1. For an explanation of the various institutions that care for and educate children in China before they enter primary school, see box 1.1 in chapter in this book.

2. In 2008, public spending on education exceeded 7 percent of GDP in Chile, Denmark, Iceland, Israel, the Republic of Korea, Norway, and the United States (OECD 2011).

3. Of the 22.4 million students in senior-secondary level TVET in 2010, 11.4 million (53 percent) received stipends of RMB1,500 ($221) a year; another 4.4 million general senior-secondary students (20 percent) also received tuition-free grants. In 2010, 4.82 million received stipends, accounting for 20 percent of the students in this subsector. No stipends were granted to them before 2010. In 2011, the stipend was made available to all students in TVET and general senior-secondary school. In higher education, 6.3 million poor students (28 percent of total enrollment) received national grants (国家助学金). The amount of the grant varied across universities, generally ranging from RMB1,500 to RMB5,000 ($221–$735) a year. Other kinds of grants, such as free tuition and meal allowances, were also provided (MOE 2011).

4. China has 22 provinces, 4 municipalities, 5 autonomous regions, and 2 special administrative regions.

References

Liu, Y. 2009. "Review of the development of China's Preprimary and Kindergarten education." Draft. China Institute for Education Finance Research, Peking University. Beijing. (中国学前教育的发展概况).

Lui, Y. and Y. Dong. 2008. "Review of OECD's Cost and Finance of Early Childhood Education." Draft. China Institute for Education Finance Research, Peking University. Beijing. (OECD国家学前教育的财政体制、资金提供机制).

MOE (Ministry of Education). Various years (including 2011). *Educational Statistics Yearbook of China*. Department of Development and Planning. Beijing: People's Education Press. (教育部发展计划司。中国教育统计年鉴。中国教育出版社。北京).

MOE (Ministry of Education), and NBS (National Bureau of Statistics). Various years. *China Educational Finance Statistical Yearbook*. Beijing: China Statistics Press. (教育部, 国家统计局。中国教育经费统计年鉴。中国统计出版社。北京).

OECD (Organisation for Economic Co-operation and Development).Various years (including 2011). *Education at a Glance*: OECD Indicators. Paris: OECD.

———. 2010a. *The High Cost of Low Educational Performance: The Long-Run Economic Impact of Improving PISA Outcomes*. Paris: OECD.

————. 2010b. *PISA 2009 Results: Executive Summary.* Paris: OECD. http://pisa2009.acer.edu.au/.

UNESCO (United Nations Educational, Scientific, and Cultural Organization). 2003. *A National Case Study of Services Provided for Children: Early Childhood Care and Education in China.* Beijing: UNESCO.

World Bank. 2009a. "China Rural Compulsory Education Finance Reform: A Case Study of Gansu." Draft. East Asia Human Development Department. World Bank, Washington, DC.

————. 2009b. "China Education Sector Review: Inputs and Suggestions to China's National Plan for Medium- and Long-Term Educational Reform and Development." Draft. East Asia Human Development Department. World Bank, Washington, DC.

Zhou, N. L. 2010. "Report on Preservice Training of Teachers of 0–3 Age Groups and 3–6 Age Groups, Regulation on kindergartens, and Facility Standards." Draft. Prepared as a background note for the World Bank. (0-3岁的早教培训, 3-6岁教师的职前培训, 幼儿园工作规程, 幼儿园建筑设计规范).

CHAPTER 4

Determinants of Child Outcomes and Policy Implications: Evidence from Hunan Province

The national-level data reported in the first three chapters reveal major rural-urban disparities in access to services and child outcomes, as well as financial constraints on the supply of and demand for services. To inform policy and design targeted interventions, additional information is needed on two empirical questions:

- How large are the disparities in weight, height, social development, and cognitive development of children between rural and urban areas, between boys and girls, between Han and ethnic minorities, and between children cared for by their own parents and "left-behind" children?
- Do enrollment in parent-child classes and kindergartens, access to health checkups, and good parenting/child-rearing practices affect weight, height, and the social and cognitive development of children, after controlling for rural and urban status, ethnicity, gender, left-behind status, educational attainment of mother and other caregivers, and family income?

A household survey was conducted in Hunan Province to collect data to answer these questions. The survey was conducted in March 2010 by the local staff of the National Population and Family Planning Commission (NPFPC), with technical assistance from the World Bank, co-financing by the NPFPC and the World Bank, and supplemental financial support from the Save the Children–China Program. Hunan was chosen because its economy is based primarily on agriculture, and its per capita GDP is at the lower-middle-income level. It thus holds lessons for agrarian-based provinces, which account for the bulk of China's population. Furthermore, as a labor-exporting province, Hunan has a sizable population of "left-behind" children. It also has several ethnic minority groups, most prominently the Miao, the Yao, and the Tujia, who are spread across other Western provinces, such as Guizhou, Yunnan, and Guangxi. It is in the national interest to promote early child development (ECD) among ethnic minorities in order to facilitate their development.

Description of Survey

The survey sampled 15 counties and urban districts. Sampling began by selecting county-level units. All county-level administrative units in Hunan were sorted into three types (first urban districts, then county-level cities, then regular counties). Within each type, counties were sorted by gross domestic product (GDP) per capita, from highest to lowest. Fifteen county-level units were then randomly selected using probability proportionate to size (PPS) sampling. As none of the 15 counties of the main sample had a heavy concentration of ethnic minorities, two minority autonomous counties were added in order to collect information on minority children and their families. The 15 counties in the main sample are referred to as "nonminority counties" in the rest of this book. The minority counties were analyzed separately; data from them were not pooled with the main sample, in order to avoid introducing bias to the mean. The total sample thus included 17 counties/urban districts and 85 villages and urban neighborhoods.

Within these villages and urban neighborhoods, 1,700 households with children between the ages of 37 and 48 months were sampled by NPFPC staff, who kept detailed records of all children born. Three-year-olds were targeted for observation, because their development status captures the development outcomes of the first 36 months of life and provides the foundation for subsequent development. Because of migration, only 1,011 households (60 percent of the original sample) were found and interviewed. No replacement was added to the sampled households. Of the households interviewed, 821 respondents in the 15 nonminority counties and 94 in the minority counties provided complete information (see annex table 4A.1 for a description of the sampling method).

The questionnaire included 208 items, which the primary caregiver (parent, grandparent, or other) answered. It included seven sections, covering the following areas:

- Basic information about the child (date of birth, birth weight and height, gender, ethnicity, rural/urban status)
- Household characteristics, including parents' marital status, parents' migration pattern, and parents' and other primary caregivers' educational attainment and occupation
- Primary caregiver's opinion on gender; childrearing practices (such as reading to the child, playing with the child, frequency of watching TV, methods of disciplining children); and attendance at parent-child classes and kindergartens
- Family conditions (including income and expenditures) and adult behavior (for example, smoking in front of the child)
- Nutrition and diet; access to medical service and health habits (for example, brushing teeth, washing hands after going to the bathroom and before meals); emotional responses in different situations; and behavioral patterns of the child
- Details on siblings and educational status
- Living conditions and household assets and debts.

The survey also measured the weight and height of children (at age 3) and included an instrument for direct observation of children by survey workers and a 47-item test of children's cognitive skills. Test items assessed whether the child could follow oral instruction (such as clapping hands or going to the door); imitate a jump and other fine motions; explain the function of certain body parts; recognize written numbers from 1 to 10; recognize a triangle, a circle, and a square; and distinguish the expression of surprise and anger when shown pictures of other children. It took about two hours to interview the caregiver and test the child.

The design of the household questionnaire was informed by other household surveys, such as the World Bank's Living Standard Measurement Survey. Questions were added on early childhood and issues associated with left-behind children. The sections on child nutrition, health, and social and cognitive development were informed by the conceptual framework presented in figure 1A.1 in the annex to chapter 1 in this book.

The team considered the technical benefits of using an internationally developed instrument in order to benchmark child development outcomes.

Attempts were made to adapt the Early Development Index (EDI).[1] However, the EDI is used to assess a population, not individuals. It is based on the assessment of kindergarten teachers. It was not appropriate for the household survey in Hunan for a variety of reasons, including the fact that the survey must be household not school based, as many 3-year-olds are not in school; unlike a teacher, the primary caregiver, who is the respondent, has no other children as reference to judge his or her child's behavior and development; and it is designed mainly for children ages 4–7 (whereas NPFPC's service targets are children age 3 and younger).

The design of the questionnaire was informed by two influential U.S. instruments, "Strengths and Difficulties" and "Ages and Stages."[2] However, because some questions were not appropriate for Chinese children (for example, whether the child can read the Latin alphabet), the research team designed its own questionnaire. Recognizing that own-designed instruments carry validity and reliability risks without expensive and lengthy testing, the team nevertheless considered it worth the risk to try out locally designed instruments, which may be culturally more appropriate.

The findings from Hunan are only suggestive, for several reasons. First, the sample is not nationally representative. Second, Hunan is a lower-middle-income province, where living conditions are much better than in arid, mountainous, or high altitude provinces in the Western region. Its ethnic minorities are more integrated with Han society and many speak Mandarin, distinguishing them from ethnic minorities in the Western region. Third, because this survey is the first of its kind, it should be treated as a work in progress. Its value lies in highlighting a number of policy issues that require attention and identifying directions for further research.

Descriptive Statistics on Household Characteristics and Habits

This section presents descriptive statistics on household and child characteristics (see annex table 4A.2 for sample mean and standard deviation of the variables analyzed). Sample means were calculated separately for the 15 nonminority counties and urban districts of the main sample and the 2 minority counties to avoid biasing the mean.

The share of the population with annual household income of more than RMB20,000 ($2,941) was 33 percent in the nonminority counties and 13 percent in the minority counties (figure 4.1). The share of the population with annual household income less than RMB2,000 ($294) was 4 percent in the nonminority counties and 9 percent in the minority counties.

Figure 4.1   Annual Household Income in Sample Counties in Hunan Province

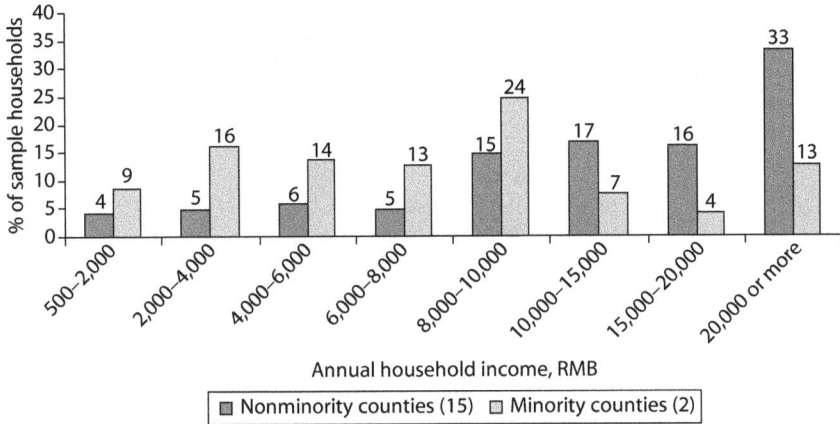

Source: Survey of Hunan Province.

The average age of children surveyed was 46.5 months old in the nonminority countries and 47.1 months in the minority counties (table 4.1). There were slighter fewer girls in the nonminority counties than in the minority counties, probably because ethnic minorities are allowed to have two to three children, reducing the propensity for gender selection. In the nonminority counties, 62 percent of respondents were rural residents, compared with 99 percent in the minority counties. In the nonminority counties, 9 percent of children were minorities; in the minority countries, 73 percent were minorities. About 69 percent of children in the nonminority counties attended nurseries or kindergartens, compared with 25 percent in the minority counties.

Left-Behind Children

In the nonminority countries, about 32 percent of 3-year-olds were left-behind children (not cared for by their mothers); in the minority counties, the figure was 48 percent. In 2009, mothers in the nonminority counties stayed home for an average 8.6 months a year; mothers in the minority counties stayed home for 6.0 months. Fathers spent less time at home, averaging 7.6 months in the nonminority counties and 5.5 months in the minority counties.

More than 90 percent of left-behind children were cared for by their grandparents, mostly by the paternal grandmother but also by the maternal

Table 4.1   Sample Mean of Characteristics of Children in Hunan Province
percent, except where otherwise indicated

Variable	Nonminority counties (15)	Minority counties (2)
Age (months)	46.5	47.1
Boys	52.5	50.3
Girls	47.5	49.7
Rural	62	99
Urban	38	1
Han	91	29
Ethnic minorities	9	73
Raised by parents	69	52
Raised by other caregivers (left-behind children)	32	48
Attended nursery/kindergarten	69	26
Did not attend nursery/kindergarten	32	76

Source: Survey of Hunan Province.

grandmother and paternal grandfather. Fathers cared for about 8 percent of left-behind children in the nonminority countries and 11 percent in the minority counties.

Grandparents bear much of the cost of raising their grandchildren. In the nonminority counties, 30 percent of caregivers did not receive any payment from their children to cover the cost of taking care of their grandchildren, 45 percent received less than RMB300 ($44) a month, 18.5 percent received RMB300–600 ($44–$88) a month, and only 7.5 percent received more than RMB600 ($88). In the minority counties, 32 percent of grandparents received no payment, and 58 percent received less than RMB300 ($44) a month.

Spending on Child Development
Lack of disposable income contrains the ability to seek health and education services and to buy books and toys that are stimulating to children. Table 4.2 shows that 41 percent of rural residents and 43 percent of minorities did not buy a single book in 2009, compared with only 8 percent of urban residents and 28 percent of Han. Minorities and rural residents also spend much less on toys.

Education of Caregivers
It is well established in the literature that the education level of the mother or other caregiver is closely associated with child development outcomes. In both samples, the educational attainment of mothers was lower

Table 4.2   Spending by Primary Caregivers in Hunan Province on Books and Toys for Children, 2009

percent

Item	Han	Minorities	Urban	Rural
Number of books purchased				
None	28	43	8	41
1–10	37	38	34	39
More than 10	35	19	58	20
Spending on toys				
None	13	10	4	16
RMB 1–100	37	50	26	45
More than RMB100	50	40	70	39

Source: Survey of Hunan Province.

than that of fathers, and that of caregivers was the lowest (figure 4.2). The educational attainment of parents and other caregivers in the minority counties was lower than in the nonminority counties. About 4.3 percent of mothers in minority counties were illiterate compared with only 1.6 percent in nonminority counties; 19 percent of caregivers in minority counties were illiterate, compared with only 9 percent in the nonminority counties. None of the mothers in the minority counties had any tertiary education, compared with 10 percent in the nonminority counties. About 54 percent of mothers in both samples had junior-secondary education; 51 percent of fathers in the nonminority counties and 70 percent in the minority counties had junior-secondary education. Only 36 percent of caregivers in the minority counties had junior-secondary education.

Language Spoken at Home
In the nonminority counties, 11 percent of respondents spoke Mandarin (standard Chinese) at home, 88 percent spoke the local dialect, and 0.7 percent spoke a minority language. In the minority counties, only 4 percent of primary caregivers spoke Mandarin, 56 percent spoke the local dialect, and 40 percent spoke a minority language.

Sources of Information on Child Development
About 95 percent of households in the nonminority counties and 92 percent in the minority counties owned a cell phone or landline. There was also a very high percentage of television ownership (98 percent in the nonminority counties and 97 percent in the minority counties).

86

Figure 4.2 Educational Level of Mothers, Fathers, and other Caregivers in Hunan Province

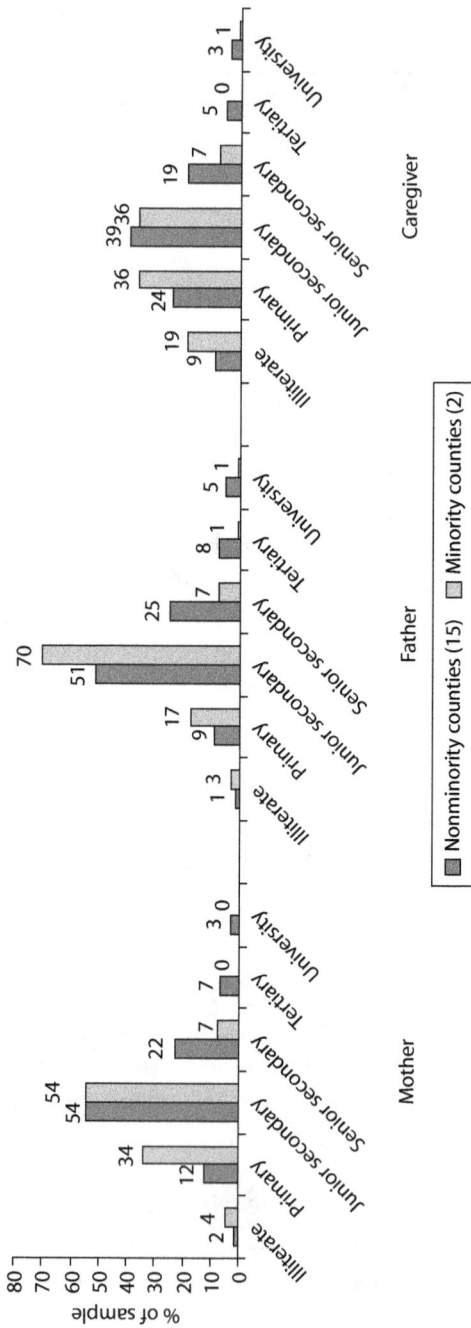

Source: Survey of Hunan Province.

For people who live in relatively isolated communities, ownership of information and communications technology provides access to information. Table 4.3 shows that 47 percent of ethnic minorities and about the same percentage of rural residents reported obtaining information about early childhood education from TV. Printed materials and friends and relatives were less important sources of information. Because television is usually broadcast in Mandarin, it has become a source for both caregivers and the children to learn the official language.

Child-Rearing Practices

There was little difference between nonminority and minority counties in the reported time spent reading to and playing with children or watching TV (figure 4.3). There was also little difference in the method of disciplining children. About 80 percent of both samples reported sometimes punishing their children; 56–60 percent said they preferred to use encouragement (figure 4.4). About an equal number of respondents in the two samples believed that girls are equal to boys.

Immunization and Health Checkups

Respondents in both samples reported similar immunization coverage, but the frequency of medical checkups varied considerably (figure 4.5). Children in the nonminority counties were checked more frequently, although only 25 percent of respondents in the nonminority counties and 15 percent in the minority counties said that their children had medical checkups annually. Children in the nonminority counties had greater access to a doctor than children in the minority counties.

Table 4.3   Channels Through Which Caregivers in Hunan Province Obtained Information about the Importance of Early Child Education

percent

Source	Han	Minorities	Urban	Rural
Television	31	47	16	43
Printed materials	27	18	37	20
Friends and relatives	13	3	11	13
Internet	1	3	2	1
All of above	20	15	31	12
Not sure	7	13	2	11

Source: Survey of Hunan Province.

Figure 4.3   Reported Percentage of Time Spent Reading and Playing with Children and Watching Television in Hunan Province

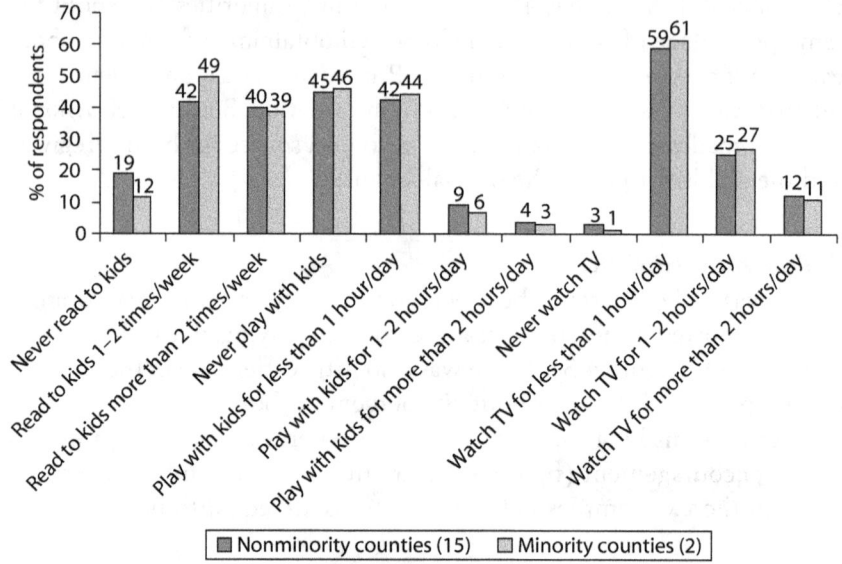

Source: Survey of Hunan Province.

Figure 4.4   Reported Method of Discipling Children in Hunan Province

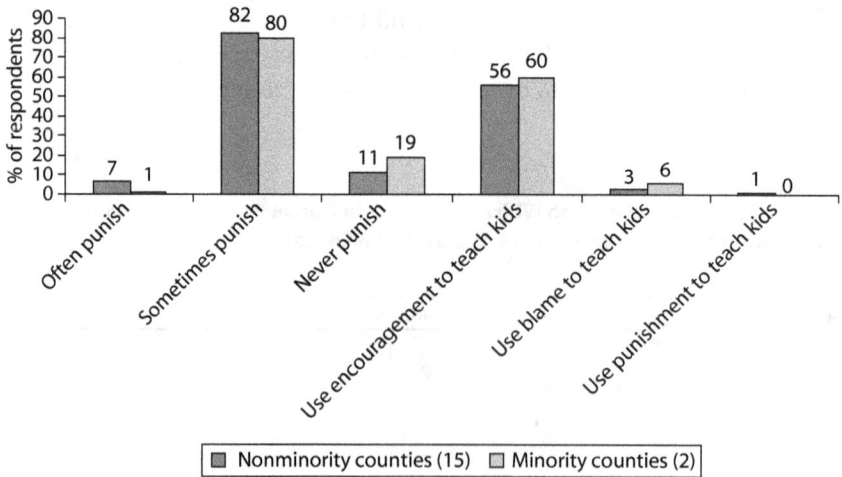

Source: Survey of Hunan Province.

Figure 4.5   Frequency of Immunization and Medical Checkups of Children at Age 3 in Hunan Province

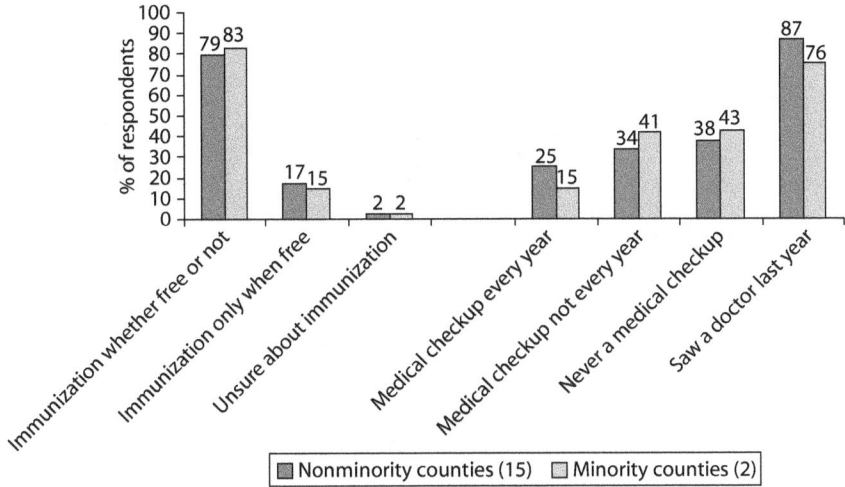

Source: Survey of Hunan Province.

Dietary Habits

Dietary differences between the two samples are striking, especially the frequency of protein intake. About 41 percent of respondents in the nonminority counties said that their children drank milk every day, compared with 27 percent in the minority counties (figure 4.6). Whereas 52 percent of respondents in the nonminority counties said that their children ate meat or eggs every day, only 20 percent of the children in the minority counties did so. About 15 percent of respondents in minority counties said that their children rarely eat meat, compared with only 8 percent of them in the nonminority counties. An almost equal percentage of respondents in both counties gave their children calcium supplements, and the vast majority of children ate vegetables every day.

Smoking

Smoking at home and in front of the child is common in China. In the nonminority counties, 71 percent of households had at least one member who smoked; 73 percent of caregivers smoked, with 81 percent of them smoking in front of the child. In the minority counties, 79 percent of households had at least one member who smoked; 55 percent of caregivers smoked, with 79 percent of them smoking in front of the child (table 4.4).

Figure 4.6   Frequency of Various Types of Food Intake by Children at Age 3 in Hunan Province

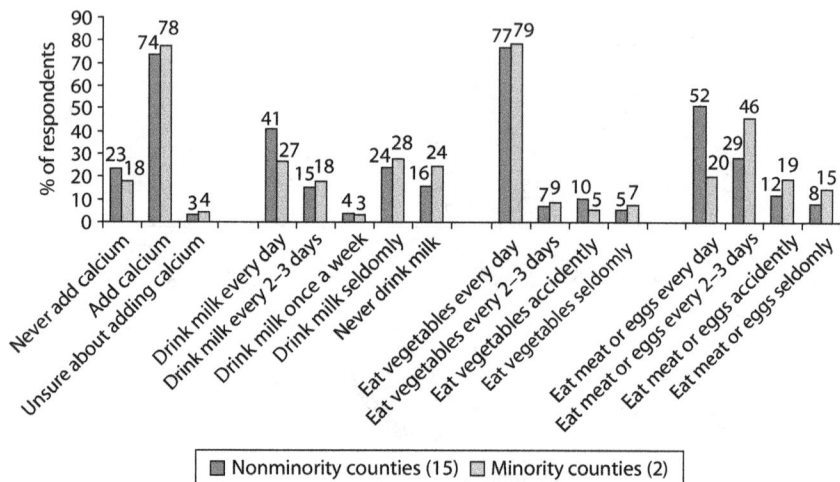

Source: Survey of Hunan Province.

Table 4.4   Prevalence of Smoking in Households in Hunan Province

	Nonminority counties (15)			Minority counties (2)		
Variable	Mean (%)	Standard deviation	Number of observations	Mean (%)	Standard deviation	Number of observations
Someone in the household smokes	70	46	800	79	41	94
1 person smokes	51	50	801	54	50	94
2 people smoke	16	37	802	18	39	94
3 people smoke	02	14	803	06	25	94
More than 3 people smoke	00	05	804	00	00	94
Caregivers smoke	73	44	805	55	50	94
Caregivers smoke in front of child	81	39	806	79	41	94

Source: Survey of Hunan Province.

The rate of smoking is high in Hunan because it is a tobacco-producing province and because many people are unaware of the effects of second-hand smoking on health. Smoking at home is unlikely to have any immediate effect on child outcomes, but it is known to have adverse effects later in life. Controlling the use of tobacco is a key way to improve health outcomes and reduce health expenditure, as well as an effective way to address the challenges of an aging population.

Table 4.5 Development Outcomes of 3-Year-Olds in Hunan Province

Variable	Nonminority counties (15)				Minority counties (2)			
	Urban		Rural		Urban		Rural	
	Mean	Standard deviation	Mean	Standard deviation	Mean	Standard deviation	Mean	Standard deviation
Boys								
Weight at age 3 (kg)	16.0	2.5	15.8	3.3	14.0	n.a.	15.4	3.9
Height at age 3 (cm)	98.9	6.0	96.7	6.1	80.0	n.a.	94.6	7.8
Social development index	3.4	0.4	3.2	0.4	3.7	n.a.	3.2	0.4
Cognitive skills	0.7	0.2	0.5	0.2	0.6	n.a.	0.5	0.2
Number of observations	299	299	487	487	1	1	93	93
Girls								
Weight at age 3 (kg)	16.0	2.5	15.7	3.5	16.1	4.3	14.6	3.2
Height at age 3 (cm)	98.1	5.9	96.9	6.4	96.1	8.2	92.7	7.3
Social development index	3.3	0.4	3.3	0.4	3.3	0.5	3.2	0.4
Cognitive skills	0.5	0.2	0.6	0.2	0.4	0.2	0.5	0.2
Number of observations	420	420	366	366	49	49	45	45
Han					**Minority**			
Weight at age 3 (kg)	15.9	3.1	15.3	2.2	16.1	4.0	15.2	3.9
Height at age 3 (cm)	97.9	5.8	94.0	8.4	94.1	5.5	94.6	8.7
Social development index	3.3	0.4	3.2	0.4	3.1	0.3	3.3	0.5

(continued next page)

Table 4.5 *(continued)*

Variable	Nonminority counties (15)				Minority counties (2)			
	Mean	*Standard deviation*	*Mean*	*Standard deviation*	*Mean*	*Standard deviation*	*Mean*	*Standard deviation*
Cognitive skills	0.6	0.2			0.5	0.2	0.5	0.2
Number of observations	719	719			25	25	69	69
	Non-left-behind children		*Left-behind children*		*Non-left-behind-children*		*Left-behind children*	
Weight at age 3 (kg)	15.9	2.9	15.8	3.2	15.4	4.0	15.4	4.0
Height at age 3 (cm)	97.6	6.3	97.5	5.8	94.6	7.3	93.3	7.7
Social development index	3.3	0.4	3.2	0.4	3.3	0.4	3.2	0.5
Cognitive skills	0.6	0.2	0.5	0.2	0.5	0.2	0.4	0.1
Number of observations	529	529	257	257	37	37	45	45
	Attends kindergarten		*Does not attend kindergarten*		*Attend kindergarten*		*Does not attend kindergarten*	
Weight at age 3 (kg)	16.2	3.2	15.1	2.5	15.6	4.4	15.3	3.8
Height at age 3 (cm)	98.3	6.2	95.9	5.7	97.8	9.9	93.4	6.9
Social development index	3.3	0.4	3.2	0.4	3.5	0.4	3.2	0.4
Cognitive skills	0.6	0.24	0.4	0.2	0.5	0.2	0.4	0.2
Number of observations	537	537	249	249	23	23	71	71

Source: Survey of Hunan Province.
Note: n.a. = not available.

Policy Questions

Do Child Development Outcomes Differ across Subgroups?

Child development outcomes were measured by weight and height, social development, and cognitive development at survey (table 4.5). Survey workers weighed and measured each child. To measure social development, they posed 29 questions to caregivers on how the child reacts and behaves in a variety of circumstances (for example, when meeting a stranger, with other children). Every question was scored on a five-point scale (never, almost never, sometimes, almost always, and always; data analysis aligned the scale to ensure that higher scores indicated better social development). Cognitive development was measured by administering a 50-item yes/no test directly to the child. The higher the aggregate score, the better the cognitive development.

Urban children, Han children, children cared for by their mother, and children who attend kindergarten were heavier and taller and had better cognitive scores, though not necessarily better social development scores, than rural children, ethnic minorities, left-behind children, and children who do not attend kindergarten. Although girls were shorter and lighter than boys, in the nonminority counties they tended to have higher social and cognitive scores. Minority girls living in the minority counties had the lowest weight and height of all groups.

What Factors Affect Child Development Outcomes?

Multivariate analysis[3] of the data in the nonminority counties was conducted to determine the effects of various variables on child development outcomes.[4] Weight, height, social development, and cognitive development were used as outcomes measures, because the determinants of these outcomes are different. For example, some children are both stunted and overweight because of malnutrition from junk food and lack of exercise. A composite of weight and height would obscure this problem. Combining social and cognitive development measures is inappropriate because children could be normal or advanced in one aspect but lag behind in the other.

Several regression models were tested. The final models are supported by theories on physical, cognitive, and social development. The mean and the standard deviation of the independent variables used are shown in table 4A.1. The regression results are presented in appendix A (at the end of the book).

Demographic Characteristics

Child age, birth weight, gender, family size, not cared for by parents (left-behind children), household income, rural resident status, ethnic minority, mother's education, and primary caregiver's education were regressed on child development outcomes. These variables are associated with family background characteristics that are not amendable to policy intervention. The adjusted R-squared statistics show that together, they explain 25–27 percent of the variance in height and weight, 11 percent of the variance in social development, and 37 percent of the variance in cognitive development. The results are reported in models 1–4 in table 4.6 and appendix A.

The main findings are as follows:

- Weight at birth was positively correlated with weight and height at age 3. Being a girl and coming from a large family were negatively correlated with weight and height at age 3.
- Height at age 3 was positively correlated with having a caregiver with at least junior-secondary education. Controlling for other characteristics, belonging to an ethnic minority had a very strong association with height, possibly indicating insufficient nutrition.
- Social development was positively associated with household income above RMB20,000, and negatively associated with family size.
- Children who lived in families with higher income, whose mothers had higher educational attainment, and whose primary caregivers had higher educational attainment had higher cognitive skills.

Other Factors Amenable to Policy Intervention

Five groups of variables that the literature has shown to be good predictors of child development outcomes were added next:

- Whether or not the child attends a nursery/kindergarten, parent-child classes, or both;
- Frequency of health check-ups;
- Parenting or child-rearing practices (frequency of playing with the child, reading to the child, watching TV, and type of disciplinary actions taken);
- Dietary habits and nutrition (frequency of eating meat and eggs, drinking milk, eating fruit and vegetables);
- Caregivers' access to child-rearing information.

These variables are more likely to be amenable to policy interventions than are family characteristics.

The main findings include the following:

- Enrollment in kindergarten is positively and statistically significantly correlated with weight, height, cognitive development, and social development. Attendance at parent-child classes also has positive effects on cognitive development. A medical checkup every year is associated with positive cognitive and social development.
- Parenting practices are important for social and cognitive development, and they likely reinforce good practices in kindergarten. The caregiver playing with the child for less than an hour a day, as opposed to not playing at all, has a statistically significant association with development. Reading to the child at least once a week is also positively related to cognitive outcomes: reading more than twice a week raises the cognitive score by 0.132 on a 2-point scale, or 0.55 standard deviation, an impact of substantial magnitude. Data from the 2009 Programme for International Student Assessment (PISA) reaffirm the importance of reading to children (Schleicher 2010): the difference in score points between 15-year-olds whose parents read to them weekly or daily when they were in primary school and those whose parents did not ranged from more than 10 points (on a 600-point scale) in Hong Kong SAR, China to more than 60 points in New Zealand (figure 4.7).[5] The difference between 15-year-olds

Figure 4.7 Differences in 2009 PISA Scores between Students Whose Parents Read to Them in Primary School and Students Whose Parents Did Not

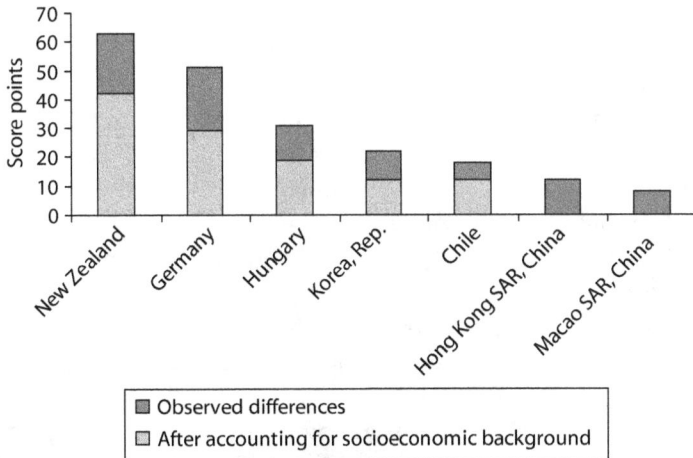

Source: Schleicher 2010.
Note: PISA is the Programme for International Student Assessment, organized by the OECD.

Figure 4.8   Differences in 2009 PISA Scores of Students Whose Parents Talked to Them about What They Did in Primary School and Students Whose Parents Did Not

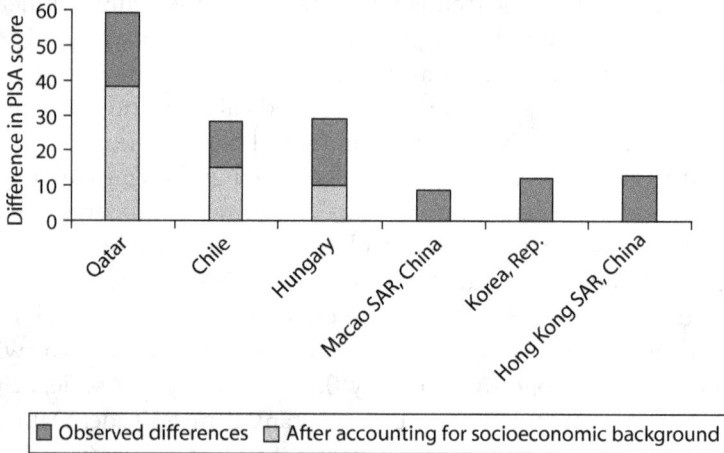

Legend: ■ Observed differences □ After accounting for socioeconomic background

Source: Schleicher 2010.
Note: PISA is the Programme for International Student Assessment, organized by the OECD.

whose parents talked with them about what they did in school and those who did not ranged from more than 10 points in Hong Kong SAR, China to 60 points in Qatar (figure 4.8).

- Watching television is positively correlated with weight, height, social development, and cognitive development at age 3.[6] The China Central Television Station (CCTV) has dedicated channels for children's programs, as do municipal and provincial stations. These programs are designed to stimulate, educate, and entertain children of all ages. The beneficial effects of TV for this age group may be akin to the Sesame Street in the United States, which successfully taught social and readiness skills (Bogatz and Ball 1971). Annex table 4A.3 describes the content of various children's programs.

- Drinking milk once a week, compared with not drinking milk, is positively correlated with height. Eating meat or eggs every day, compared with rarely, is positively correlated with weight. Kindergarten attendance also has a positive association with weight and height, possibly because kindergartens provide meals and snacks that may compensate for the lack of certain nutrients at home.

- Caregivers who obtain information from television, as compared with other sources, such as newspapers, magazines, or word of mouth, tend to have children with better cognitive outcomes, after controlling for other effects, suggesting that parenting education can improve child development outcomes.

The adjusted R-squared statistics of these variables (models 5–8) are higher than those of models 1–4 (table 4.6 and appendix A.1). Model 8 explains about 47 percent of the variance in cognitive scores, up from 37 percent in model 4.

Policy Implications

The Hunan data provide some good news. The fact that age, rural resident status, household income, and "left-behind" status have no statistically significant association with weight and height suggests that children's basic needs are being met in Hunan Province. However, Hunan is a lower-middle-income province in China, not a poor one. It would be wrong, to generalize the findings from Hunan to poorer provinces. In 2008, for example, the percentage of stunted children under age 5 was 47 percent in Guangnan County in Yunnan, 42 percent in Jiangxi County in Guangxi, 24 percent in Menyuan County in Qinghai, and 23 percent in Anshun County in Guizhou, according to the Report of China Food and Nutrition Surveillance System (Chen 2009). In these extremely poor counties, the determinants of weight and height are likely to be very different.

After adding the variables of access to services and parenting or child-rearing practices in the multivariate analysis, household income and mother's education no longer had statistically significant effects on weight, height, and social development, and the effects of caregiver's education declined. The effects of household income of RMB6,000–RMB 15,000 ($870–$2,173) had no statistically significant association with children's cognitive skills. The statistical significance of mother's education also disappeared; only caregiver's education above junior-secondary level had statistically significant effects on cognitive development.

These results suggest that the effects of mothers' and caregivers' education and household income are exerted through access to ECD services and good child-rearing practices. Providing these services and information to influence child-rearing practices can alter the inherent inequity of childhood experience and improve physical, social, and cognitive development. Given that birth weight is an important predictor of weight and height at age 3, ensuring proper prenatal nutrition can help improve physical development. The fact that birth weight affects all subsequent weight and height makes a strong case for improving prenatal care and nutrition for pregnant women in order to ensure better child outcomes after birth.

Table 4.6 Independent Variables with Statistically Significant Associations with Child Outcomes in Hunan Province

Variable	Demographic characteristics without other predictors				Access to early childhood development and education and health services, child-rearing practices, and dietary habits, controlling for demographics characteristics			
	(1) Weight	(2) Height	(3) Social scores	(4) Cognitive scores	(5) Weight	(6) Height	(7) Social scores	(8) Cognitive scores
Birth weight	+	+	+		+	+		
Female	−	−			−	−		+
Family size			−	+			−	
Household income (compared with income below RMB 2000)								
RMB 2,000–RMB 6,000				+				+
RMB 15,000–RMB 20,000				+				+
More than RMB 20,000			+	+				
Minority		+				+		
Mother's education (compared with illiteracy)								
More than three-year college				+				
Caregiver's education (compared with illiteracy)								
Primary				+				
Junior-secondary		+		+		+		+
Senior-secondary				+		+		
Three-year college						+		
University				+	+			
Attend kindergarten					+	+		+
Attend parent-child classes							+	+

	(1)	(2)	(3)	(4)	(5)	(6)	(7)	(8)
Read to child (compared with no reading)								
More than once a week								+
More than twice a week								+
Play with child (compared with no play)								
Less than 1 hour/week							+	
Obtain information on early childhood education and development from television (compared with from other sources)							+	+
Child watches TV (compared with rarely)								
Less than 1 hour/day						+	+	+
1–2 hours/day						+	+	+
More than 2 hours/day						+	+	+
Medical checkup every year (compared with rarely)							+	+
Drinks milk once a week (compared with not)						+		
Eats meat or egg every day (compared with rarely)					+			
Constant	13.173	90.731	2.924	0.098	9.642	97.321	3.558	0.533
R-Squared	0.33	0.35	0.21	0.44	0.37	0.40	0.25	0.56
Adjusted R-squared	0.25	0.27	0.11	0.37	0.26	0.30	0.12	0.47
Number of observations	803	803	803	803	786	786	786	786

Source: Survey of Hunan Province.

Note: + indicates positive correlation. – indicates negative correlation.

Annex 4A Sampling of the Hunan Household Survey

The sample covered 1,700 households in 17 counties in Hunan, including 2 ethnic minority–autonomous counties, in order to oversample minorities. Within each county, 5 village-level units (the equivalent of a district in urban areas) were surveyed; within each unit, 20 households with children 37–48 months old were surveyed.

Sampling began by selecting the counties. All counties in Hunan were first sorted into three types (first urban districts, then county-level cities, then regular counties). Within each type, counties were sorted by GDP per capita from highest to lowest. Probability proportionate to size (PPS) sampling was then employed. A cumulative population for each county was calculated by adding the population of each county to the population of all counties above it (after sorting the list as described above). A sampling interval was chosen by dividing the total population by the number of sampled counties. At first, 15 counties were selected. A random number between 0 and 1 was multiplied by the sampling interval to obtain a random starting point. The county containing the cumulative population greater than but closest to the starting point was chosen as the first county. The next county was then selected by adding the sampling interval to the starting point and choosing the county whose cumulative population was greater than and closest to that sum. Remaining counties were chosen in the same fashion. Two minority autonomous counties were added after the first 15 counties to ensure that the sample included a sufficient number of ethnic minority children.

In each county-level unit, five village-level units were sampled randomly using PPS sampling, where size was measured by population. There was no stratification at the village level. The villages were chosen using the sample PPS command in STATA.

In each village-level unit (including urban neighborhoods), 20 households with children 37–48 months old were randomly sampled. In cases where the number of households with 3-year-olds was less than 20, all households in the villages were sampled, because otherwise there would be no replacements if the selected households did not want to or were unable to respond. Local staff of the National Population and Family Planning Commission (NPFPC) prepared the list of households for random selection. If the main caretakers of children could not be found or refused to participate in the survey, they were not replaced in the sample.

Field testing was conducted in October 2009 and again in February 2010. A three-day training was conducted in March 2010. The survey was administered by 120 NPFPC staff, supported by a team from the Education Department of East China Normal University.

Table 4A.1   Mean and Standard Deviation of Independent Variables in Hunan Household Survey

Variable	Mean	Standard deviation
Child's weight at age 3 (kg)	15.90	3.07
Child's height at age 3 [cm]	97.55	6.24
Child's social development measurement (5-point scale, higher being better)	3.26	0.39
Child's cognitive skill measurement (2-point scale, higher being better)	0.56	0.24
Child's age (months)	46.46	6.49
Child's weight at birth (kg)	6.59	0.97
Child's gender (female)	0.47	0.50
Child's family size (number of persons)	4.39	1.35
Child not raised by parents	0.34	0.47
Household income Y 500–Y 2000	0.04	0.19
Household income Y 2,000–Y 4,000	0.05	0.22
Household income Y 4,000–Y 6,000	0.06	0.24
Household income Y 6,000–Y 8,000	0.05	0.21
Household income Y 8,000–Y 10,000	0.15	0.35
Household income Y 10,000–Y 15,000	0.17	0.37
Household income Y 15,000–Y 20,000	0.16	0.36
Household income Y 20,000 or above	0.34	0.47
Rural region	0.62	0.48
Minority	0.09	0.28
Mother's education = illiterate	0.02	0.12
Mother's education = primary school	0.12	0.33
Mother's education = junior-secondary school	0.54	0.50
Mother's education = senior-secondary school	0.23	0.42

(continued next page)

Table 4A.1   *(continued)*

Variable	Mean	Standard deviation
Mother's education = three-year college	0.07	0.25
Mother's education = four-year college or above	0.03	0.18
Caregiver's education = illiterate	0.09	0.29
Caregiver's education = primary school	0.24	0.43
Caregiver's education = junior-secondary school	0.39	0.49
Caregiver's education = senior-secondary school	0.19	0.39
Caregiver's education = three-year college	0.06	0.23
Caregiver's education = four-year college or above	0.03	0.18
Respondent never reads to child	0.19	0.39
Respondent reads to child 1–2 times a week	0.42	0.49
Respondent reads to child more than twice a week	0.40	0.49
Respondent never plays with child	0.45	0.50
Respondent plays with child less than 1 hour a day	0.42	0.49
Respondent plays with child 1–2 hours a day	0.09	0.29
Respondent plays with child more than 2 hours a day	0.04	0.19
Respondent often punishes child	0.07	0.26
Respondent sometimes punishes child	0.82	0.39
Respondent never punishes child	0.11	0.31
Respondent doesn't care about punishment	0.01	0.07
Child attends kindergarten	0.68	0.47
Parent and child attend parent-child class	0.19	0.39
Child has medical checkup every year	0.25	0.43
Child does not have medical checkup every year	0.34	0.47
Child never has medical checkup	0.37	0.48
Respondent unsure about medical checkup	0.03	0.18
Child never watches TV	0.03	0.18
Child watches TV less than 1 hour a day	0.60	0.49
Child watches TV 1–2 hours a day	0.25	0.43
Child watches TV more than 2 hours a day	0.12	0.33
Child eats meat or eggs every day	0.52	0.50
Child eats meat or eggs every 2–3 days	0.28	0.45
Child eats meat or eggs occasionally	0.12	0.33

Table 4A.1   *(continued)*

Variable	Mean	Standard deviation
Child eats meat or eggs rarely	0.08	0.27
Child drinks milk every day	0.41	0.49
Child drinks milk every 2–3 days	0.15	0.36
Child drinks milk once a week	0.04	0.20
Child drinks milk rarely	0.24	0.43
Child never drinks milk	0.16	0.37
Child eats fruit every day	0.50	0.50
Child eats fruit every 2–3 days	0.21	0.41
Child eats fruit occasionally	0.21	0.41
Child eats fruit rarely	0.08	0.27
Respondent never adds calcium to child's diet	0.24	0.42
Respondent adds calcium to child's diet	0.74	0.44
Respondent unsure about adding calcium to child's diet	0.03	0.17
Child is immunized whether immunization is free or not	0.79	0.41
Child is immunized only when immunization is free	0.18	0.38
Child is never immunized	0.02	0.14
Respondent unsure about immunization	0.02	0.12

Source: Authors.
Note: Number of observations = 800; Y = Chinese Yuan (RMB); the mean for most variables is a percentage (e.g., 0.47 = 47%), unless specified.

Annex 4B Television Programs for Children and Youth in China

Four channels in China aim to educate children through entertainment and cultivate their self-confidence and interest. On the whole, these are healthy programs. Programming is important in China, where TV often acts as a substitute parent/caregiver in educating children.

Central Television Station

Channel CCTV-15 is dedicated to programming for children and youth. It began broadcasting December 28, 2008. Its core operating principle is respect for children's rights. It seeks to help children and youth develop their full potential, provide guidance for their healthy development, and provide a happy living space for them. Programming aims to be healthy, interesting, good for cognitive development, and educational.

Main programs include the following:

06:00 Cartoon City: Little Friends' playground
06:30 Big Windmill (TV magazine for youth)
07:00 Happy Sky Flipping Cartoons
08:00 Silver River Drama
09:00 Cartoon Dream Workshop
09:30 Open Sesame: Scientific Playground
10:00 Cartoon City: Little Friends' Playground
10:30 Little Wisdom Tree: Integrating education with play
11:00 Happy Sky Flipping Cartoons
13:30 Wisdom Speed Car

Beijing TV Channel for Children
Beijing municipality has its own TV channel and special programs for children. Examples of its programming are as follows:

06:19 Cartoon
06:42 Mobilization of Toys
06:50 Digital Baby
08:20 Precious Fruit Special
08:50–12.50 Happy Lamb and Grey Wolf
12:50 Mobilization of Toys
12:55 The World of Cartoons
13:25–14.25 Classical Cartoons
14:25–17:00 Dragon King Warrior of Dinosaur Baby
17:00 Made in China: Kungfu Panda
17:30: Soccer Player of the Song Dynasty

Shanghai Oriental Channel for Children
Shanghai Municipality has its own program for children. "Happy Jumping" is a very popular and influential program designed for children ages 3–6. Since it began broadcasting, in March 1996, it has aired more than 800 episodes. In July 2004, it became an official children's channel.

The program's objective is to cultivate brave, self-confident, and expressive children. This goal is reflected in the program's slogan, "No need for rehearsal, every child is a good actor."

The program uses play in a happy setting to develop children's creativity and imagination and build confidence, based on the following ideas:

- Children tell the truth: They express their own view of life and build their self-confidence.
- Jumping and hopping: Physical exercise, accompanied by music, allows children to stretch and expend their energy.
- You ask and I answer: Dialogue between children and between children and parents puts children on an equal basis with parents, facilitating their understanding and trust.
- Playing and games: Self-created games let children do what they normally do not do. Through these games, they acquire knowledge and establish the concept of physical effort, both of which make them more confident and creative.

Hunan Golden Eagle Cartoon
Hunan province, like other provinces, has its own TV channels and special programming for children. Below are some examples:

07:00 Roll Call for Flying
07:15 Happy Party
07:25 Adventure of Star Fox or Water Baby's 10,000 Why?
07:45 Playing Names
08:00 Happy Du Du
12:00 The Adventure of Lolo
12:50 Models from East and West
13:20 Kungfu Mobilization
13:30 The Adventure of Naja
16:15 Name Game
16:30 Happy Party
17:00 Cartoon Mountain Cat
17:30 Flying Playground
18:00 Electronic Boy
18:30 Iron Dragon
19:00 Ocean Baby Is Coming
19:45 Name Game
20:00 Mechanical Animal God
21:00 Flying Story House

Notes

1. The Early Development Index (EDI) is a child development outcome measure devised by Janus and Offord (2000) as a teacher-completed measure of five aspects of early child development relevant to children's successful transition into school. Teachers complete a checklist for all children in their class on five developmental domains: physical health and well-being, social competence, emotional maturity, language and cognitive development and communication skills, and general knowledge. This instrument has been shown to be a reliable, valid, and effective means of population-level monitoring of the outcome of children's development in their first five years of life.

2. Ages and Stages Questionnaires are used for developmental and social-emotional screening of children from 1 month to 5 and one-half years old, mostly in the United States. Highly reliable and valid, they are used by professionals (such as pediatricians and Head Start staff) and parents to identify a child's strengths, trouble spots, and developmental milestones (www.agesandstages.com). Strengths and Difficulties Questionnaires are behavioral screening instrument for children ages 3–16. Several versions of the questionnaires are available to meet the needs of mental health clinicians, educators, and researchers. Each version includes 25 items on psychological attributes (emotional, conduct, hyperactivity/inattention, peer relationship, and prosocial behavior) to be completed by parents/teachers and by adolescents; an impact supplement; and follow-up questions on whether the interventions were useful (www.sdqinfo.com).

3. The equation of the multivariate analysis is as follows:

$$Y_{ihc} = \alpha_0 + \alpha_1 \times X_{ihc} + \alpha_2 \times \mathbf{X}_{hc} + \gamma_c + \varepsilon_{ihc},$$

where Y_{ihc} is the outcome variable of child i living in household h in community c; X_{ihc} is a vector including individual level variables for child i living in household h in community c; X_{hc} is a vector including household level variables for household h in community c; γ_c are community fixed effects, represented by a series of community dummies; and ε_{ihc} is an error term with mean equal to zero.

4. Because of the small size of the sample in the two minority counties, separate regressions could not be run for them. Although it is theoretically possible to use the population as a sample weight and pool the two samples, the lack of population data in urban districts convinced the study team to restrict the analysis to the main sample, which is representative of Hunan Province.

5. The PISA is an international assessment by the OECD of achievement in mathematics, science, and reading by 15-year-olds in both member and non-member states. Started in 2000, the international assessments are conducted every three years to inform policy and practices in education. The 2009 assessment tested 470,000 students in 65 countries in 2009 and another

50,000 students in 9 countries in 2010. The municipality of Shanghai (with a population of 20 million people) participated for the first time, placing first in all three areas.

6. In older children, too much television watching may encourage intellectual passivity and damage eyesight. Thus, it is important not to generalize the findings of this study of young children in Hunan to a broader population.

References

Squires, J., and D. Bricker. 2009. *Ages and Stages Questionnaires*, 3rd ed. Baltimore, MD: Paul H. Brookes Publishing Co. http://www.agesandstages.com.

Bogatz, G. A., and S. Ball. 1971. *The Second Year of Sesame Street: A Continuing Evaluation.* New York: Children's Television Workshop. Princeton, NJ: Educational Testing Service, Princeton, NJ.

CDRF (China Development Research Foundation). 2011. CDRF Program on Early Childhood Development: Qinghai Pilot Interim Report. CDRF, Beijing.

Goodman, R. 1999. *Strengths and Difficulties Questionnaires.* http://www.sdqinfo .com.

Janus, M., and D. Offord. 2000. "Readiness to Learn at School." *Canadian Journal of Policy Research* 1 (2): 71–75.

Schleicher, A. 2010. Presentation on Programme for International Student Assessment (PISA) before U.S. Congress, December 7. http://pisa2009.acer .edu.au/.

CHAPTER 5

The Way Forward

The challenge of early child development (ECD) in rural China is mammoth. Of the 16 million babies born in China every year, 61 percent live in rural areas, where conditions are often inauspicious for development. In 2008, slightly more than a third of babies suffered from anemia at 6 months. In poor rural counties, up to 21 percent of 2-year-olds were stunted. A third of rural 3-year-olds had been left behind by their migrant parents, cared for by other caregivers, most often grandmothers, who usually have less education and are less well informed about nutrition, health, and education than the parents. Only about a third of rural children enroll in kindergarten and preprimary school, with a third of those children attending only a single year of preschool class rather than several years of kindergartens.[1]

Given the enormous social benefits and high economic returns of ECD—in the form of higher educational attainment and productivity and lower probability of antisocial behavior— failing to provide ECD is very costly indeed. Moreover, given China's aging population, rising inequality, and massive migration, which weakens family structure, there is an urgency to undertake measures to improve the quality of early development, in order to ensure that younger generations are able to sustain development.

The government of China recognizes that achieving the goals of social harmony, political stability, and economic prosperity requires breaking the intergenerational transmission of poverty by providing integrated ECD services. Toward that end, the 12th Five-Year Plan (2011–15) emphasizes improvement of people's livelihood (NPC and CPPCC 2011). The government amplified and reinforced its position in its subsequent promulgation of a series of guidelines on the development of women and children, reduction of rural poverty, improvement of services for the elderly, extensions of the health system, and measures to increase the well-being of the population (State Council 2011a, 2011b, 2011c, 2011d, 2011e, 2011f, 2012).[2] These documents consistently include references to people with disabilities and ethnic minorities as groups facing unique challenges and deserving special assistance. (See annex table 5A.1 for key indicators of well-being under the 12th Five-Year Plan, annex table 5A.2 for the targets to be achieved in education, annex table 5A.3 for recommendations on the development of preprimary education, annex table 5A.4 for the measures for women's development, annex table 5A.5 for the measures for children's development, and annex table 5A.6 for the measures to reduce poverty and develop rural areas).

The government is to be commended for moving in the right direction and addressing issues in a timely, coherent, and systematic manner. Because its guidelines specify implementation, monitoring and evaluation, and accountability for achieving the targets, they are in a better position to influence resource allocation from the center to provinces, from provinces to counties, and within counties. As services are provided at the local level, the guidelines are likely to affect how local governments prioritize their spending. If all annual performance reviews also include measures taken, the level of resources available, the extent to which targets have been met, and service receivers' feedback, officials at all levels will face strong incentives to pay special attention to early child development, women's development, and poverty reduction.

The 12th Five-Year Plan period marks a turning point in early child development. Accomplishments of its goals and targets will affect what is possible in the 13th Five Year Plan and whether China can attain the status of a *xiao kang* (or "well off") society by 2020—a society in which the basic needs of all members (food, clothing, housing, education, health care, social insurance, and old age pension and care) will be met.

Targeting ECD services to the most disadvantaged groups—people in extreme poverty, people with disabilities, and ethnic minorities—should command a high priority. The central government's poverty reduction program provides earmarked funds targeting interventions to the extremely poor. A second priority would be to expand the provision of ECD services in rural areas through the regular budgetary process under line ministries and their counterparts in provincial and local governments, supported by central fiscal transfers in the Western and Central regions. For both options, there is a need to distinguish services for children ages 0–3 from services for children ages 3–6, whose developmental needs differ.

Early Child Development as Part of the Government's Program to Reduce Poverty

To realize its development objectives, China must give top priority to extremely poor children, in order to change the trajectory of their lives. In 2009, there were 36 million extremely poor people in China (people earning less than RMB1,196 ($1,760) a year, far below the government's new poverty line of RMB2,300 ($366). These people have large families: two-thirds of them have five or more family members, and 18 percent (6.5 million) are children under the age of 12. Because children are covered by free compulsory education after reaching the age of 6 or 7, the estimated 3–4 million extremely poor children age 6 and under should be the prime beneficiaries of services (NBS 2009a).

Geographic targeting is possible because two-thirds of the extremely poor live in the Western region, 25 percent in the Central region, 5 percent in the Eastern region, and 3 percent in the Northeastern region (NBS 2009a). Provinces in the Western and Central areas performed far worse than provinces elsewhere in terms of maternal mortality, the percentage of babies born with low birth weight, under-5 mortality, and student-to-staff ratios at ECDE centers. The incidence of poverty among ethnic minorities, who tend to live in the hard to reach, remote, mountainous areas, is 11 percent, twice the national average. The *Guidelines on Poverty Reduction and Rural Development (2011–2020)* (State Council 2011c) prioritizes contiguous mountainous areas for targeted assistance.

The government's poverty reduction program has been targeting 592 poor counties (about 21 percent of all counties in China) for special assistance and monitoring. Activities include improvement of the means of production (agriculture, forestry, livestock raising, and processing of agricultural products); improvement of infrastructure (land, drinking water for people and animals, roads, electricity, telecommunication, schools, and health clinics); and training and education. In 2009, of the RMB36.7 billion ($5.4 billion) allocated for poverty reduction, 45 percent was spent on improvement of the means of production and 32 percent on infrastructure improvement; just 1.8 percent went to social services, including education and training.

Before the 12th Five-Year Plan, the poverty reduction program did not include ECD services for extremely poor children ages 0–6 or monitor their access to services, although it did monitor enrollment in compulsory education for children ages 6–15 (NBS 2009a).[3] One of the key targets of the poverty reduction and rural development plan (2011–20) is to achieve, by 2015, 80 percent enrollment of children in three-year programs before entering grade 1(see annex table 5A.6). This change represents a major step forward.

The next two subsections describe good practices for the care and education of children ages 0–3 and 3–6 and review cost-effective service delivery mechanisms in the light of international experience.

Interventions for Children Ages 0–3

Services to children ages 0–3 include safe shelter, nutrition, basic health care (immunization, oral rehydration therapy, and hygiene), and age-appropriate language, motor and sensory stimulation, and protection from physical danger.

The determinants of healthy development of children ages 0–3 are adequate nutrition (including breastfeeding and complementary feeding), management of various childhood illnesses (such as diarrhea), health and hygiene practices, the quality of interaction between the mother/caregiver and the child, immunization, sensory motor and language stimulation, and opportunities for play and exploration. Desirable outcomes are freedom from intermittent diseases, nutritional security, curiosity, sociability, the confidence that comes from appropriate self-help, and development of sensory motor skills and language skills. Indicators are full immunization against major diseases, appropriate height and weight for age, age-appropriate gross and fine motor skills and auditory visual skills, ability to communicate clearly and confidently, and sociability (see annex figure 1A.1 in chapter 1 in this book for the conceptual framework of child development from ages 0–6).

The evidence from Hunan, which shows the predictive power of birth weight on weight and height at age 3, and from the pilot study by China's Center for Disease Prevention and Control's on the effects of nutritional interventions on physical and cognitive growth (box 5.1)

Box 5.1

Strategy on Nutritional Security Recommended by China's Center for Disease Prevention and Control

China's Center for Disease Prevention and Control (CDC) piloted a study in five poor counties that examined 1,500 children divided into a treatment group and a control group. Babies 6- to 12-months-old in the treatment group were given a nutritional sachet every day until they were 24-months-old. The formula of the nutrition package included 10 grams of whole soybean powder, fortified with 6 milligrams of iron, 4.1 milligrams of zinc, 385 milligrams of calcium, 0.2 milligrams of vitamin B2, and 280 international units of vitamin D3. At 24 months, the prevalence of anemia in the treatment group was 45 percent lower than in the control group, the children were 1.3 centimeters taller, and their development quotient score was 1.7–3.4 points higher. A follow-up study found that the differences in intelligence score were sustained through age 6, with the development quotient scores of the treatment group 3.1–4.5 score higher than the scores of the control group.

The CDC advocates the inclusion of the following components into China's social and economic development plan and poverty alleviation plan:

- Introduction of complementary feeding for poor children
- Establishment of a national food fortification program
- Scaling up of the provision of effective fortified food products for pregnant women and children under age 2
- Establishment of an indicator system for nutrition security (such as the prevalence of stunting and anemia among children at age 3 or among pregnant women).

It also supports the integration of several indicators into the national statistical report.

Source: Chen 2009.

make a compelling case for nutrition and health interventions. Interventions for extremely poor people should include the following components:

- Free prenatal care, nutrition, and information for pregnant women in order to increase safe delivery and the health of the baby;
- Subsidies for transportation of poor women for routine health checkups and for hospital delivery;

- Provision of free nutritional dense food packages that include protein, iron, calcium, and other micronutrients for children 6–36 months old;
- Free routine health care and immunization for children under age 6;
- Prenatal and postnatal classes for mothers to enhance their knowledge and skills in complementary food preparation, feeding practices, and parenting techniques; and
- The formation of networks of caregivers in local communities to share experience and create opportunities for children to interact with their peers.

Given that 90 percent of children under the age of 2 in China are cared for at home, parenting education is critical to improve child development outcomes. Parenting education can be provided to mothers, fathers, and other caregivers, such as grandparents. It typically teaches the techniques of human interaction needed for emotional, social, and cognitive development. It also provides counseling to address specific issues at home. Parenting training usually encourages caregivers to play with, read to, and teach their children basic concepts, such as numbers, shapes, and colors. It also encourages them to take children to play in groups and to create opportunities for peer interactions, which are essential for developing social and language skills.

The Ministry of Health foresaw the need to intervene in this area. On May 2, 2012, it issued a series of technical notes providing instruction on how to inspect newborn babies, conduct health checkups of children, improve child nutrition, and manage nutritional diseases (MOH 2012). For its part, the Ministry of Education announced piloting of ECD service for children 0–3 in selected areas (MOE 2012).

A home-based and community-based approach that facilitates interaction and training of mothers and caregivers by people knowledgeable about nutrition, health, and stimulation can be highly cost-effective. The Social Assistance Department within the Ministry of Civil Affairs (MOCA) is considering introducing a child-focused component into the minimum guarantee scheme (*dibao*) or possibly a conditional cash transfer. MOCA's Social Welfare Department plans to pilot community-based delivery of a comprehensive child welfare service package. MOCA is also considering scaling up the training of social workers to support community-based service delivery. For its part, the State Council's Leading Group on Poverty is piloting community-based services for poor children.

International experience shows that these mechanisms are affordable, cost-effective, and sustainable. The annual cost per child of a home visiting program is $90 in Morocco, $113 in Mexico, and $312 in Jamaica (Naudeau and others 2011). Examples of community- or home-based programs are described in table 5.1.

Interventions for Children Ages 3–6

A child's development follows a general pattern, notwithstanding the fact that the process will vary from individual to individual, and culture to culture. During ages 3–6, children's coordination is relatively well developed, and cognitive development and pre-literacy skills occur rapidly. Age-appropriate developmental interventions would include engaging in simple problem solving tasks, developing self-care skills, social skills (interacting with other children and with adults), and associating the written with the spoken language.

The Ministry of Education operates a formal system of kindergartens for children ages 3–6. However, it underserves rural children, particularly extremely poor children living in remote areas. Given the high cost of center-based ECD services such as parent-child classes and formal kindergartens, local governments in rural areas are unlikely to have sufficient revenue to fund center-based ECD services. The financial constraints of local government limit supply, and parental inability to pay dampens demand.

Expansion of ECD services need not replicate the formal model of provision, however. Services can be provided in a flexible manner. Kindergarten provides up to 8–10 hours of services a day (40–60 hours a week), including daily breakfast, snacks, lunch, and a two-hour afternoon nap. Reducing the length of the day could reduce costs, allowing children to be accommodated in two shifts in the same facility, perhaps even taught by the same teachers.

A review of the international literature finds that children, in particular poor children from at-risk socioeconomic backgrounds, are likely to benefit from participating in center-based development programs. Intensity and dose effects are correlated with positive outcomes Alternative modes of delivery could use parenting education to deliver curriculum-based information at home (tables 5.2 and 5.3).

The emerging evidence of the cost-effectiveness of ECD in breaking the intergenerational transmission of poverty has convinced a growing number of countries to provide services to the poor. Latin America is particularly advanced in experimenting with instruments (box 5.3).

Table 5.1   Examples of Community- or Home-Based Child Development Programs in Selected Countries

	Progam description
Brazil	Early childhood program offers childcare on Saturdays, coupled with parent training in health and education. Training classes use videos and discussion to cover a range of areas, from specific health interventions ("How to treat infant diarrhea") to stimulating playtime ("The world of make-believe!").
Jamaica	Home-based program uses stimulation to mitigate effects of stunting. Stunted children 9–24 months old were given nutritional supplements of 1 kilogram of milk-based formula per week and stimulation through one-hour weekly home visits by community health workers to improve mother-child interactions through play. After two years of intervention, the gap in the development quotient between stunted and nonstunted children was narrowed. Follow-up study of these children at ages 7–8, 11–12, and 17–18 found that the cognitive and educational performance of children receiving stimulation improved over time. Among children who received nutritional supplement but not stimulation, the positive cognitive effects ceased to be evident at ages 11 and 17 (Grantham McGregor and others 1997).
Mexico	Preschool expansion policy included mandate for all parents to send their 3-, 4-, and 5-year-old children to preschool. In 2005, coverage reached 98 percent of 5-year-olds, 81 percent of 4-year-olds, and 25 percent of 3-year-olds. The target was for 100 percent coverage of 5-year-olds in 2004, 4-year-olds in 2005, and 3-year-olds in 2008 (these targets have yet to be met). Mexico expanded the program to provide low-cost but high-quality parenting education for all children under the age of 4 (for details, see box 5.2).
Nepal	Discussions among village women were facilitated on various issues related to childbirth and child care. These groups formulated and implemented strategies to generate community funds for maternal and infant care and organized home visits to newly pregnant women by a group member. In the process, program participants sought and received information on maternal and child health and care. Impact evaluation of program found lower neonatal death rate, higher uptake of prenatal and delivery services, and improved home care practices in program communities than in control communities. Similar results were found in the trial of this approach in the Warmi Project in Bolivia.
Vietnam	Home-based program provides nutrition to children under age 3 and stimulation for 4- and 5-year-olds. Evaluation found improved cognitive outcomes compared with children who received only the nutrition intervention.

Source: Naudeau and others 2011.

Box 5.2

Helping Parents Stimulate Early Child Development in Mexico

Mexico's Consejo Nacional para el Fomento Educativo (CONAFE) developed a low-cost model to reach 8 million children under the age of 4. The model uses existing infrastructure, such as preschools and public spaces, for meeting areas to enable a network of volunteers to teach parenting education classes in target communities. The parenting training aims to improve children's competencies and school readiness. Preliminary evidence reports that 80 percent of teachers and 76 percent of school directors find greater parental attention and support provided by parents who participated in CONAFE's program. In addition, almost 87 percent of parents reported that their children had made an easier-than-expected transition to preschool as a direct result of the program. The cost is $112 per child per year, allowing the government to serve large numbers of the target group in a sustainable manner.

Training sessions and activities for parents and caregivers, their young children, and pregnant women aim to strengthen family understanding of early child development and demonstrate how the family can best stimulate the process. Each parent education session follows a didactic approach consisting of four phases: reflection, sharing ideas, practice, and closing and is supported by program materials provided by CONAFE. Evaluations are integrated into the program cycle at the beginning (3 sessions), periodically during the course of the year (4 sessions), and at the conclusion (1 session). A trained promoter provides 18 weekly two-hour sessions to families with children ages 0-4 years, eight monthly two-hour sessions to mothers, and eight monthly two-hour sessions to expectant mothers, during nine-month yearly cycles.

The program offers two innovations: early stimulation activities working directly with children (together with their parents) and parenting education directed toward fathers. The project supports 18 weekly 2-hour early stimulation sessions for children under age 2 accompanied by their parents and 5 special 2-hour sessions aimed at fathers. These sessions promote father's participation in childrearing. Education creates a space for them to share and learn among their peers.

Source: Holland and Evans 2010.

Table 5.2   Effects of Parenting Education on Child Outcomes in Turkey, the United States, and the United Kingdom

Country	Effect
Turkey	The Turkish Early Enrichment Project provided a two-year parenting information program to mothers of 3- to 5-year-olds. Some of these children attended a preschool, some attended a custodial day care center, and some stayed home. Program included biweekly home visits and group meetings on alternate weeks to provide training and support. Using a curriculum based on the HIPPY (Home Instruction Program for Preschool Youngsters [see table 5.3]) program, every week mothers were supplied with learning materials and instruction on how to use the materials with their children. Group meetings consisted of guided discussions on various topics, such as nutrition, child health, play activities, discipline, and child-parent communication. The early advantage of children in educational preschools, who had higher baseline IQ and cognitive and social-emotional measures than those in custodial day care or home care, dissipated by the fifth year of primary school. In contrast, the effects of parenting information programs on children's school achievement and socioemotional development and social adjustments were sustained throughout childhood.
United Kingdom	A large-scale longitudinal study of home activities in the United Kingdom found that reading to children; providing them with opportunities to play with numbers, paint, and draw; and teaching them letters and numbers had significantly positive effects on the level of literacy and numeracy at age 5.
United States	Learning opportunities provided at home (for example, frequently being read stories and visiting libraries or museums) were positively associated with school readiness.

Source: Naudeau and others 2011.

Early Child Development as a Mainstream Service

ECD interventions that reduce income and social gaps between poor and nonpoor populations are multisectoral in nature, including health, nutrition, education, water, hygiene, sanitation, environmental protection, and legal protection. To make ECD a mainstream service, policy makers need to establish a framework that provides vision and sets targets. Different policy areas that affect young children should be linked; coordinated efforts can be made across multiple line ministries and their local counterparts toward a common set of outcomes. Responsibilities for children under age 3 are diffused in China, making the need for a policy framework acute.

Table 5.3 Curriculum-Based Parenting Education Programs in the United States

Program	Goal	Entry and exit	Main inputs
DARE to Be You	Improve parenting skills and child development in ways that contribute to children's resiliency to substance use later in life.	2–5 years	Parent-child workshops with focus on parenting skills and developmentally appropriate children's activities (15–18 hours of parent training workshops and simultaneous children's programs, preferably over 10- to 12-week period)
HIPPY (Home Instruction Program for Preschool Youngsters)	Help parents with limited education prepare their children for school entry.	Entry: 3–4 years Exit: 5 years	Parenting classes and books given to parents with activities to do with children; home visits enable parents to meet with paraprofessionals weekly for 45–60 minutes; parents meet with children using HIPPY materials at least 15 minutes a day; parents have group meetings monthly. Program runs 30 weeks a year for two years.
Incredible Years	Promote child social and emotional competence and address children's behavioral and emotional problems.	2–8 years	Parenting classes and children's programs; parents attend classes 2 hours a week for 12–14 weeks, children attend classes 2 hours a week for 18–20 weeks.
Parents as Teachers	Empower parents to give their children a good start in life, prepare children for school entry, and prevent and reduce child abuse.	Entry: Before birth up to 8 months Exit: 3–6 years	Home visits by parent educators; group meetings with parents; developmental health, vision, and hearing screening; and building of networks to meet family needs; weekly to monthly home visits/group meetings of 60–90 minutes each.

Source: Naudeau and others 2011.

Box 5.3

Experience of ECD in Latin America

Middle-income countries in Latin America and the Caribbean use ECDE to

• Enhance children's cognitive and socioemotional development, physical growth, and well-being
• Enhance prenatal care with services and information, to increase the probability of delivery of a healthy baby
• Educate parents and caregivers in better parenting, health, and hygiene practice and provide them with the opportunity to work.

   Impact evaluation of programs in the region has reached the following conclusions:

• Conditional cash transfer programs in Mexico have had large positive effects on the physical development of young children. Chile's program has improved the probability that young children attend preschool. Nicaragua's program has reduced developmental delays.
• Parenting programs in Bolivia, Honduras, Jamaica, and Nicaragua have helped parents improve their child-rearing and child stimulation techniques, resulting in improved development of cognitive, language, motor, social, and other skills.
• Early education and preschool programs in Argentina and Uruguay have raised children's language and math test scores, improved their behavioral skills, and had positive effects on long-term educational attainment.
• Nutrition and supplementation programs targeted to low-income children—such as Mexico's subsidized milk programs for children and pregnant and lactating women, Colombia and Guatemala's nutrition and early child care programs, and conditional cash transfer programs in Mexico and Colombia—have improved cognitive outcomes and the physical well-being of children. Interventions that offer nutrition supplements, together with interventions that combine several strategies (for example, parenting practices, early childhood care, and nutrition) have had positive effects on children's acquisition of language, reasoning, vocabulary, and schooling.
• Programs that condition cash payment on children's attendance at health centers and periodic physical monitoring—such as the programs in Colombia, Honduras, and Mexico—have had beneficial impacts on health. Ecuador's unconditional cash transfer program appears to have had positive effects on the development of children's motor skills and other developmental indicators, mainly because of better household nutrition and deworming medications.

Source: Vegas and Santibañez 2010.

Policy Framework

International experience suggests that a national ECD policy should achieve the following:

- Define an institutional anchor and achieve intersectoral coordination.
- Ensure adequate funding (by, for example, creating a dedicated national fund, using existing social funds or budgets, or instituting fee-sharing schemes or earmarked taxes).
- Define core priorities, such as whether policies will be targeted or universal, which populations take priority, and what proportion of funds will be allocated to ECD activities.
- Build on the success of existing interventions, based on rigorous evaluations and cost accounting.
- Ensure coherence with other related policies from inception. Create a set of monitoring indicators to measure progress toward the goal and provide the foundation for an accountability mechanism.

Funding Mechanism

China's National Plan Outline for Medium- and Long-term Education Reform and Development aims to vastly expand preprimary education. Barring major changes, the decentralized financing structure is likely to perpetuate existing inequities. Central fiscal transfers along the model of transfers for compulsory education are needed to expand services in rural areas, particularly to the Western and Central provinces, where the needs are greatest. A policy framework would guide the allocation of funds and activities.

Alternatives to reaching the hard to reach. In general, in rural areas that are not extremely poor, in which most women have access to a hospital for delivery, and in which children are not malnourished, parenting education for mothers and other caregivers should be the top priority, because the quality of their daily interaction affects child development most. Parenting education needs to address some common practices that are detrimental to child development (a prime example is smoking in the presence of children). Parenting education is important even if children are attending kindergarten, as complementary quality inputs are far more effective than stand-alone efforts. Television, which is critical in disseminating information on child-rearing practices, could be used more effectively to convey parenting information, and children's programs could be more educational, strengthening the concepts of vocabulary development, health, science, and good social behavior. The marginal cost of these complementary activities is likely to be low.

It is useful to examine policies of the Organisation of Economic Co-operation and Development (OECD) that are pro-poor and pro-family and children. Almost all OECD countries have some form of subsidies for low-income families to enable them to access ECDE services (table 5.4).

Given that China has a fairly high rate of labor force participation of women, a more pro-family policy is likely to release the ingenuity and efforts of half of the workforce. Lessons can be learned from the experiences of Cuba and Sweden (box 5.4).

Conclusion

The relatively small size of the 0–6 age cohort, the low child dependency ratio, and increasing urbanization create favorable conditions for investing in ECD in China (figures 5.1 and 5.2). That said, the rollout of many important social programs, such as health insurance, pension, and free compulsory education, is placing an enormous burden on county finances.

Table 5.4   Policies Toward Children Ages 3–6 in Countries of the Organisation of Economic Co-operation and Development

Country	Partial subsidy of tuition fees	Subsidies for low-income families with multiple children	Partial exemption from tuition fees	Partial exemption of fees at some childcare centers
Australia	✓	✓		✓
Belgium	✓		✓	✓
Canada	✓			✓
Denmark	✓	✓		✓
Finland	✓			✓
France	✓	✓	✓	✓
Italy				✓
Korea, Rep.	✓	✓	✓	✓
Luxembourg			✓	✓
Netherlands	✓	✓		✓
Norway	✓	✓		✓
Portugal		✓	✓	
Sweden			✓	✓
United Kingdom	✓	✓	✓	✓
United States		✓	✓	✓

Source: Liu and Dong 2008.

Box 5.4

Equity and Child Development in Cuba and Sweden

Despite major differences in their economic conditions, political systems, and income levels, both Cuba and Sweden have done a good job in providing services for children.

Cuba

In contrast to all other Latin America countries—and despite its low level of income—Cuba has attained a high level of literacy. Children in Cuba have the highest test scores for 3rd grade achievement in language and math in Latin American and the Caribbean. Although preschool is not compulsory, it is an initial link and part of a nationwide system of education. Comprehensive programs target children ages 0–5, enrolling about 98 percent of this age group. Services include formal daycare centers and informal programs. Parents are engaged through the message "Educate Your Child," which begins in families and communities and links to enrollment of 5- to 6-year-old children in preschool preparatory programs.

The attention given to children in Cuba begins during pregnancy, when women receive a special allocation of milk and staple foods. Parenting programs are available for mothers and families. As soon as children are born and until they enter primary school, they benefit from an array of childcare and early child development services, all of which involve parents and communities (the informal sector) and health and education institutions (the formal sector). Services are intergenerational—for example, a literacy program for parents is linked with development strategies for their children.

Sweden

Sweden provides a continuum of services for children from birth to age 6. Two percent of Sweden's GDP goes to expenditures for family welfare. These expenditures include care and education in the preschool system beginning at age 1.

Preschool education is voluntary, but 95 percent of children under age 6 participate. The system aims to encourage learning and provide a safe environment for children of parents who work or study. Its overall goal is to "educare." The curriculum focuses on the meaning of facts (not facts per se), thematic learning (rather than subject learning), and play-based activities related to the learning process.

(continued next page)

Box 5.4 *(continued)*

The Swedish government sets guidelines and regulations for the preschool system, and the country's 290 municipalities finance and provide services. Preschool is integrated into the rest of the school system as the first level of education. Quality is maintained through governance. Sweden's legal and regulatory framework for preschool services ensures fair and sustained investment in these services, and substantive research serves as the foundation for curriculum and professional development.

Source: Countries' experiences summarized by the authors.

Figure 5.1   Population Age Structure of China, 1953–2008

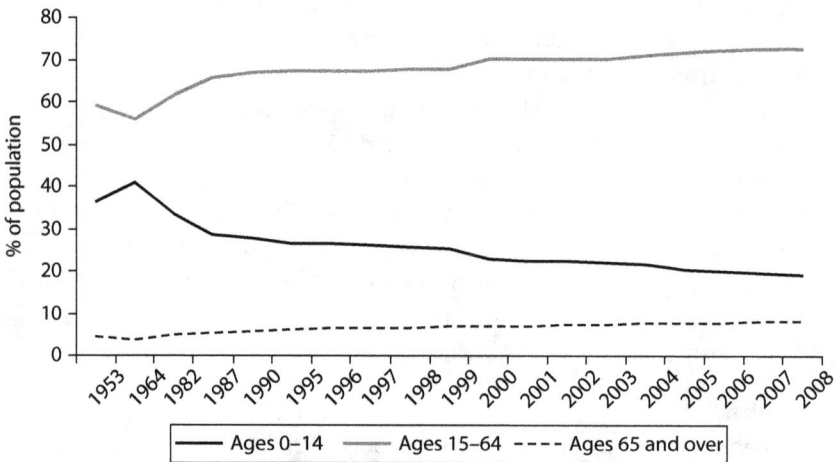

Source: NBS 2009c.

This book supports the government's additional fiscal transfers to the Western and Central areas to support local governments in the provision of cost-effective community- and home-based ECD services instead of expensive kindergartens. Evaluation of various pilots of services to children ages 0–3 and 3–6 would inform the government on how to scale up the interventions. Special attention needs to be paid to capacity building,

Figure 5.2   Rural and Urban Population in China, 1952–2008

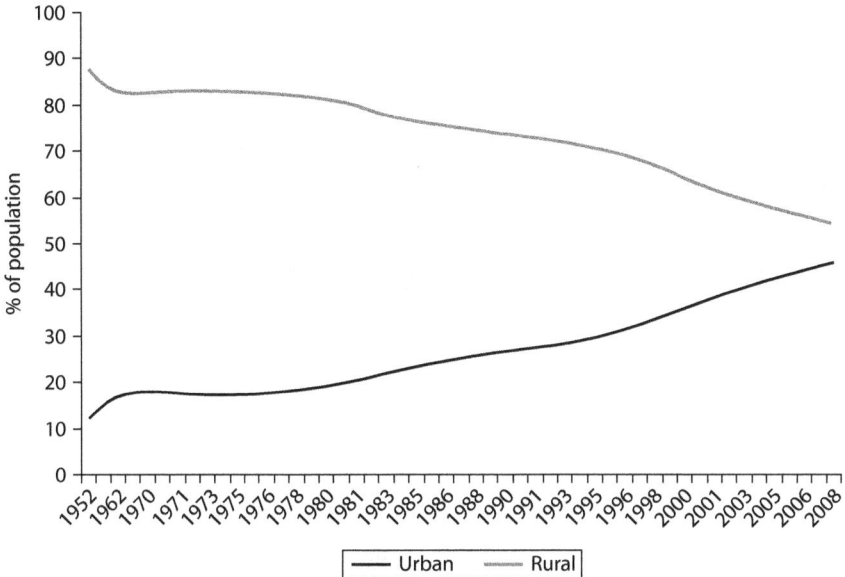

Source: NBS 2009c.

particularly that of rural and ethnic minority communities, so that they can deliver integrated nutritional, health, and early stimulation/education services effectively. Pilots could test a variety of interventions appropriate for various types of terrain and geographic locations. The role of the central and provincial government in providing financial and technical support to these communities is critical to success. Priority targeting of children at risk—children in remote areas, ethnic minorities, and left-behind babies and toddlers—could be followed by universal coverage in the future.

Improving the quality of human capital lies in the critical path of China's ascension to a high-income economy. Children under age 6 today will enter the labor force in 2030. Investing in them now will enable China to overcome the challenges of an aging population, improve the competitiveness of its workforce, and transition to a knowledge-based economy. Investing in ECD is the next frontier for breaking the intergenerational transmission of poverty and improving national competitiveness in the years to come.

Annex 5A State Council Polices and Guidelines on Education, Poverty Reduction, and Development of Women and Children

Table 5A.1   Selected Key Indicators of Well-Being During the 12th Five-Year Plan

Indicator	2010	2015	Annual growth
Average per capita income of urban resident	RMB19109 ($2,810)	> RMB26,818 ($4,271)	> 7%
Average per capita income of rural resident	RMB5,919 ($870)	> RMB8,310 ($1,323)	> 7%
Participants in old-age insurance[a]	257 million	357 million	—
Total population	1.34 billion	1.39 billion	—
Life expectancy (years of age)	73.5	74.5	

Source: NPC and CPPCC 2011.

Note: Exchange rate of RMB6.2787 = $1 (set by People's Bank of China, April 27, 2012) was used. —— = not available. a. China's social protection program comprises three major components: social insurance, social assistance, and pension. Social insurance covers basic old age insurance among urban enterprise employees (223 million participants in 2009); unemployment insurance (120 million participants in 2009); work injury insurance (140 million participants in 2009); and maternity insurance (80 million participants in 2009). Social assistance, which is the backbone of China's social safety net and a tool in crisis response, is the minimum income guarantee, known as *dibao*. In 2009, urban *dibao* provided 23.5 million beneficiaries with RMB227.8 ($33.30) per month; rural *dibao* provided 47.6 million beneficiaries with RMB100.8 ($14.70) per month. Pensions for rural and urban areas were piloted to cover people above the age of 65 (World Bank 2010a).

Table 5A.2   Achieved and Targeted Gross Enrollment Ratios in China, by Subsector, 2009–2020

Level of education/target	2009	2015	2020
Early childhood education			
Number of children in kindergarten or preprimary class (millions)	26.6	34.0	40.0
Gross enrollment ratio (GER) for children entering kindergarten or preprimary class one year before starting grade 1 (%)	74.0	85.0	95.0
GER for children entering kindergarten two years before starting grade 1 (%)	65.0	70.0	80.0
GER for children kindergarten three years before starting grade 1 (%)	50.9	60.0	70.0
Compulsory education (grades 1–9 [Primary and junior-secondary school])			
Number of students (millions)	157.7	161.0	165.0
School retention rate (%)	90.8	93.0	95.0

(continued next page)

Table 5A.2 *(continued)*

Level of education/target	2009	2015	2020
Senior-secondary education (grades 10–12, including students in technical and vocational schools)			
Number of students (millions)	46.2	45.0	47.0
GER (%)	79.2	87.0	90.0
Technical and vocational education			
Number of students in secondary technical and vocational schools (millions)	21.8	22.5	23.5
Number of students in higher vocational colleges (millions)	12.8	13.9	14.8
Higher education (including higher vocational colleges and universities)			
Number of students (millions)	29.8	`33.5	35.5
Of which undergraduates (millions)	28.3	30.8	33.0
Of which graduate students (millions)	1.40	1.7	2.0
GER (%)	24.2	36.0	40.0
Continuing education			
Number of on-the-job learners in further or continuing education (million person-times)	166.0	290.0	350.0
Goals for human resource development			
Number of people with higher education (millions)	98.3	145.0	195.0
Average education of working-age (20–59) population (years)	9.5	10.5	11.2
Share of working-age population with higher education (%)	9.9	15.0	20.0
Average education of new entrants to workforce (years)	12.4	13.3	13.5
Share of new entrants with at least senior-middle school education (%)	67.0	87.0	90.0

Source: State Council 2010a.

Table 5A.3   Recommendations for Improving Preprimary Education Under the 12th Five-Year Plan

Area	Recommendations
Prioritization of preprimary education	• Preprimary education is the beginning of lifelong learning. It establishes the foundation for the individual, the family, and the nation. Yet it is the weakest subsector of education in China, because of inadequate finance, weak institutions, insufficient number of teachers, and rural and urban disparity. • Preprimary education is a public good that deserves priority in policy intervention. • Preprimary education should be accessible to the public. The difficulty of gaining admission to kindergarten should be resolved.

(continued next page)

Table 5A.3   *(continued)*

Area	Recommendations
Expansion of services and diversification of provision	• The government will invest in building new kindergartens, converting other buildings to be used as kindergartens, and extending existing schools to provide preprimary education. • The government will provide incentives to communities, collectives, and the private sector to operate affordable kindergartens by making land available, reducing rent, and providing tax benefits. • The government can send public sector teachers to work in privately operated kindergartens. • The government welcomes private sector provisions for kindergarten and will facilitate the registration, licensing, and evaluation of private kindergartens. • The government will expand in-service and preservice teacher training. • In localities without kindergartens, higher levels of government will not approve plans for land use if they do not include locations for kindergartens. • Building kindergartens in rural areas will become an integral part of the building of a new socialist countryside (an existing program to modernize and upgrade social services in rural areas). • Investment priority will be given to the Western and Central regions of China to set up kindergartens and make available instructional materials, toys, children's books, and teachers to improve services.
Strengthening of kindergarten teachers	• Enrollment in teacher training institutions will be increased. • University graduates will be recruited into preprimary education (by giving extra training on ECD if they are not specialized in this subsector). • Teacher education in ECD will be made free of charge (in contrast to other disciplines). • Extra support will be provided to teachers in remote areas. • In-service training will be provided to 10,000 kindergarten principals and key teachers over a three-year period. • All kindergarten principals and teachers in the country will have received training.
Diversification of resources	• Public expenditures on preprimary education will be increased. • Preprimary education will be funded on a cost-sharing basis with households. • Public subsidies will be provided to children with disabilities, orphans, abandoned children, and children from poor families to enable them to attend kindergarten.
Regulation and management	• The government will regulate the licensing, certification, and evaluation of kindergartens to ensure that they provide high-quality education and meet health and safety standards.

(continued next page)

Table 5A.3   *(continued)*

Area	Recommendations
Supervision and monitoring	• There will be clear delineation of responsibilities for supervision and monitoring for different levels of government and agencies.
Regulation of fees	• Fees will be regulated according to the 2011 *Regulation on Kindergarten Fees*. • Different levels of government will set fees based on the local economy and the ability of households to pay. • Information on fees will be made public to prevent overcharging.
Care and curriculum content	• Kindergartens will provide care and education based on scientific findings and in accordance with the 2010 *Guidelines on Curricular Content of Preprimary Education*. • Learning should be activity based and experiential. • Kindergartens should provide a rich and joyful environment. They are prohibited from teaching the primary school curriculum. • Research networks will be formed to support preprimary education. • A system of quality assurance will be set up.
Leadership and coordination	• The relevant authority in the central government will set standards and use research to support preprimary education. • Various ministries and lower-level governments will support expansion and improvement of preprimary education, in land use, locality planning, teacher training, the environment, health, recruitment and promotion, and social protection.

Source: State Council 2010b.

Table 5A.4   Key Targets and Measures for Women's Development, 2011–20

Sector	Targets and measures
Health	• Reduce the maternal mortality ratio to 20 deaths per 100,000 live births in 2015 (from 26 per 100,000 in 2011). • Increase coverage for regular cervical pap smear screening and breast examination to 80 percent. • Control sexually transmitted diseases and HIV/AIDS. • Raise awareness of psychological and mental health. • Reduce anemia among pregnant women. • Ensure the right to family planning and the use of contraception. • Increase hospital delivery to 98 percent nationwide and 96 percent in rural areas.
Education	• Enroll 70 percent of girls in kindergartens three years before entering grade 1.

(continued next page)

Table 5A.4   *(continued)*

Sector	Targets and measures
	• Increase school retention rates among girls to 95 percent. • Raise the gross enrollment ratio in higher education to 40 percent among women. • Train students for employment. • Raise the average number of years of education of women in the work force to 11.2. • Reduce female illiteracy rate to less than 2 percent. • Use continuing education and distance education to upgrade skills. • Encourage women to enter the field of science.
Economic participation	• Eliminate discrimination in the workplace. • Increase the share of women to 40 percent of the work force. • Reduce income inequality between men and women (enforce equal work for equal pay). • Raise the share of women in high-level technical and professional positions to 35 percent. • Reduce poverty among women. • Affirm women's right to own land and operate businesses.
Political participation, leadership, and management	• Promote political representation of women in local and national congress. • Recruit and promote women to positions of leadership. • Appoint more women to boards of enterprises, trade unions, housing committees, village committees, and other positions of power.
Social protection	• Make medical insurance and unemployment insurance available to more women. • Raise the coverage of older women with pensions/social security to 90 percent. • Provide income subsidies and rehabilitation services to women with disabilities.
Environment	• Increase the share of the population with access to clean drinking water to 85 percent. • Increase the share of villages with separate toilet facilities for men and women to 85 percent. • Support women during natural disasters. • Use mass media to promote the principle of gender equality and raise women's self-confidence, self-reliance, and sense of their own rights. • Raise women's consciousness of the need to save energy and reduce their carbon imprint. • Promote family education to raise men's sense of shared responsibilities within the family and to strengthen family life. • Encourage women to participate in international exchanges.

(continued next page)

Table 5A.4   *(continued)*

Sector	Targets and measures
Legal protection	• Pass and enforce antidiscrimination laws. • Enforce anticrime laws and heavily penalize prostitution, abduction, and violence against women. • Discourage sexual harassment in the workplace. • Protect property rights within the family. • Provide legal aid to women. • Encourage women to enter the legal profession, and appoint women as judges and prosecutors.
Implementation of measures to support women's development	• Direct various levels of governments and agencies to make action plans and coordinate efforts. • Form national networks to implement policies in favor of women's development. • Increase public investment to support measures that promote women's development, particularly in poor and ethnic minority areas, and integrate investments into the budgetary process.
Monitoring and evaluation	• Require various levels of government to provide midterm and final reports on the status of implementation. • Collect, analyze, and report statistics to monitor outcomes.

Source: State Council 2011b.

Table 5A.5   Key Targets and Measures for Children's Development, 2011–20

Sector	Targets and measures
Health[a]	• Reduce the infant mortality rate from 13 deaths per 1,000 live births in 2010 to 10 by 2015. • Reduce the under-five mortality rate from 16 deaths per 1,000 live births in 2010 to 13 per 1,000 in 2015. • Reduce the number of babies born with birth defects. • Reduce disability caused by injury and disease. • Control the transmission of communicable disease, such as HIV/AIDS, sexually transmitted diseases, tuberculosis, and hepatitis B. • Increase immunization coverage to 95 percent. • Reduce the tetanus rate to less than 1 percent. • Reduce the incidence of low birth weight to less than 4 percent. • Increase the incidence of breastfeeding of babies during first six months of life to 50 percent. • Reduce the prevalence of anemia in children under 5 to 12 percent. • Reduce the prevalence of anemia in primary and secondary school children by one-third. • Reduce the prevalence of poor eyesight, dental disease, obesity, and malnutrition among children. • Reduce the prevalence of mental and psychological diseases. • Raise awareness of reproductive health among children at an appropriate age.

(continued next page)

Table 5A.5   *(continued)*

Sector	Targets and measures
Education	• Integrate child development in health and early stimulation for children ages 0–3. • Raise the share of children entering kindergarten three years before grade 1 to 70 percent. • Raise the share of children entering kindergarten/preschool classes one year before entering grade 1 to 95 percent. • Raise enrollment in senior-secondary education to 90 percent. • Reduce rural/urban disparity in the quality of education. • Support education in ethnic minority areas, respect the right of minorities to use their own language in preprimary education, and strengthen teacher training in minority communities. • Establish one public central kindergarten in every township, one independent kindergarten in every large village, and a satellite kindergarten in smaller villages. • Use mobile teachers in sparsely populated areas to provide guidance in preprimary education. • Provide subsidies to families with children with special needs. • Improve the boarding system in compulsory education to meet the needs of children left behind by their migrant parents. • Assign responsibility to the government in host areas to provide education to migrant children. • Ensure that children with disabilities receive compulsory education and have access to preprimary and postcompulsory education by either integrating them in regular schools or building special schools where the need is justified. • Ensure that orphans, street children, children with HIV/AIDS, and children of inmates receive compulsory education and have access to postcompulsory education. • Protect orphans and abandoned children by housing them in foster homes or welfare institutes.
Welfare[b]	• Guarantee children the right to medical services. • Entitle children ages 0–6 with disabilities with the right to rehabilitation. • Provide children with chronic illness with subsidies and nutritional supplementation. • Increase boarding subsidies to poor families. • Register children with disabilities and street children to ensure their protection.
Social environment	• Increase the share of cities and communities with service centers to provide integrated recreation, education, medical, and psychological support and referral to 90 percent. • Ensure that centers to support families and provide counseling are established in 90 percent of cities and 80 percent of administrative villages.

(continued next page)

Table 5A.5   *(continued)*

Sector	Targets and measures
	• Entitle parents to counseling on family life/education twice a year, and encourage them to participate in activities twice a year.
	• Strengthen research on family life education.
	• Promote better parent-child relationships, and prevent domestic violence and neglect.
	• Establish a healthy cultural environment by promoting children's literature, TV programs, songs, plays, dance, drama, cartoons, games, and extracurricular activities.
	• Promote healthy use of the Internet, and prevent children's addiction to Internet games.
	• Encourage children to participate in community affairs and public service.
	• Prohibit sex-selection abortion.
	• Promote the rights of girls.
Administration and management	• Direct various levels of governments and agencies to make action plans.
	• Assign a lead agency to be responsible for child development and to coordinate and supervise multisectoral efforts and report results.
	• Increase public investment to support measures that promote child development, particularly in poor and ethnic minority areas.
	• Integrate the resource needed into the budget to ensure that the mandate is funded.
Monitoring and evaluation	• Require the responsible officials to provide midterm and final reports on the status of implementation.
	• Collect, analyze, and report statistics to monitor outcomes.

Source: State Council 2011b.

a. The health targets are to be achieved by massively investing in maternal and child health, particularly in rural and remote areas; strengthening the service network among counties, townships, and villages; monitoring the growth of newborns; integrating early child development for children ages 0–3; making host areas responsible for providing services to migrant children; providing premarital counseling, prenatal nutrition, and checkups for pregnant women; treating communicable diseases; using mass media to raise consciousness and knowledge about maternal and child health; promoting safety measures to prevent drowning, injury, and traffic accidents; raising awareness of the importance of sleep, rest, recreation, nutrition, and the negative effects of smoking, alcohol, and narcotics; providing psychological counseling in school; protecting water sources from industrial pollution; and monitoring toy and food safety.

b. The concept of children's welfare has been changed from support for targeted groups to entitlement of children to receive education, medical care, protection, and equal opportunity for employment.

Table 5A.6 Key Targets in the Government's Poverty Reduction and Rural Development Programs, 2011–20

Sector	2015	2020
Agriculture	Improve agriculture and irrigation to ensure food security.	Improve agriculture infrastructure and production.
Development of production utilizing comparative advantage	Increase each household's income through improving at least one means of production.	Establish a system of production using comparative advantage.
Drinking water	Problem basically solved	Provide piped water for all.
Electricity	Massively reduce the number of people without electricity.	Provide electricity to entire population.
Transport	Raise the ratio of Class 2 highways to other roads in poor counties; raise the share of paved roads to 80 percent in all administrative villages (Tibet exempted from this target).	Expand paved roads in administrative villages, increase public transportation and rail transport.
Housing	Rebuild 800,000 dilapidated houses.	Improve housing in poor counties.
Preprimary education	Raise the gross enrollment ratio to 80% for three years of preprimary education before grade 1.	Universalize preprimary education.
Senior-secondary education	Raise the gross enrollment ratio in senior-secondary education to 80 percent.	Universalize senior-secondary education.
Literacy and training	Eradicate illiteracy, raise technical skills through training, and expand skill training for transition to other jobs.	Spur the rapid development of distance and community education.
Health	Complete the establishment of service networks at the county, township, and village levels; increase the capacity of personnel; establish one government clinic and one doctor per township and one health post per village; raise the participation rate among new rural cooperatives to 90 percent; and progressively raise child health and control communicable diseases.	Ensure that all people in poor areas have access to health care.
Culture and media	Ensure that all villages with more than 20 households have TV broadcast and that every county has a digital cinema; ensure that all administrative villages have broadband, covering all natural villages (lowest-level community), and transport networks.	Complete the network of TV broadcast, broadband, public libraries, and cultural centers in all natural villages.
Social protection	Increase minimum protection.	Increase pension coverage to 100 percent.
Population	Contain natural increase to 8 percent and total fertility rate to 1.8.	—
Forestry	Increase forest coverage by 1.5 percent.	Increase forest coverage by an additional 3.5 percent.
Migration	Facilitate migration from unsustainable areas.	—

Source: State Council 2011e.
Note: — = not available.

Notes

1. For an explanation of the various institutions that care for and educate children in China before they enter primary school, see box 1.1 in chapter 1 in this book.

2. Extensions of the health system under the 12th Five-Year Plan include free immunizations; health checkups of children, pregnant women, and the elderly; and treatment of communicable diseases, high blood pressure, and serious mental illness.

3. Evaluation by the World Bank in Gansu Province and the Basic Education in Western Areas Project confirmed that the abolition of miscellaneous and textbook fees and the provision of boarding subsidies since 2006 in the Western areas and nationwide after 2008 have contributed to increased enrollment, retention, and achievement of children in compulsory education, particularly girls and minorities (World Bank 2009a, 2009b, and 2010b).

References

McGregor, Grantham S. M., S. P. Walker, S. M. Chang, and C. A. Powell. 1997. "Effects of Early Childhood Supplementation with and without Stimulation on Later Development in Stunted Jamaican Children." *American Journal of Clinical Nutrition* 66: 247–53.

MOE (Ministry of Education). 2012. *Piloting of Services to Children 0–3.* Document No. 8. Beijing: MOE. http://www.moe.gov.cn/publicfiles/business/htmlfiles/moe/s3327/201204/xxgk_134850.html (教育部。开展0-3岁婴幼儿早期教育试点工作)

MOH (Ministry of Health). 2012. *Technical Instructions on Care, Nutrition, and Health of New Born Babies and Children.* Document No. 49. Beijing: MOE. www.moe.gov.cn/publicfiles/business/htmlfiles/moe/s3327/201204/xxgk_134850.html (卫生部。开展0-3岁婴幼儿早期教育试点工作)

Holland, P., and D. Evans. 2010. "Early Childhood Development Operations in LCR: Jamaica, Mexico, and Brazil in Focus." En Breve 152, Washington, DC: World Bank. http://www.worldbank.org/enbreve.

Lui, Y. and Y. Dong. 2008. "Review of OECD's Cost and Finance of Early Childhood Education." Draft. China Institute for Education Finance Research, Peking University. Beijing. (OECD国家学前教育的财政体制、资金提供机制)

Naudeau, S., N. Kataoka, A. Valario, M. J. Neuman, and L. K. Elder. 2011. *Investing in Young Children: An Early Childhood Development Guide for Policy Dialogue and Project Preparation.* Directions in Development. Washington, DC: World Bank.

NBS (National Bureau of Statistics of China). 2009a. *Poverty Monitoring of Rural China*. Beijing: China Statistics Press. (国家统计局。中国农村减贫监测报告. 中国统计出版社。北京)

———. 2009b. *China Statistical Yearbook*. Beijing: China Statistics Press. (国家统计局。中国统计年鉴。中国统计出版社。北京)

———. 2009c. *China Population and Employment Statistics Yearbook*. Department of Population and Employment Statistics. Beijing: China Statistics Press. (国家统计局。中国人口和就业统计年鉴。中国统计出版社。北京)

Nelson, C. 2011. "Neural Development and Lifelong Plasticity." In *Nature and Nurture in Early Child Development*, ed. D. P. Keating. New York: Cambridge University Press.

NPC (National People's Congress), and CPPCC (Chinese People's Political Consultative Conference). 2011. *Outline of the Twelfth Five Year Plan of Economic and Social Development of China*. Beijing. http://www.gov.cn/2011h/content_1825838.htm. (全国人民代表大会和中国人民政治协商会议。中国国民经济和社会发展第十二个五年规划纲要)

State Council. 2010a. *China's National Plan Outline for Medium- and Long-Term Education Reform and Development 2010–2020*. Beijing: State Council. http://www.gov.cn/jizg/2010-07/29. (国务院。国家中长期教育改革和发展规划纲要)

———. 2010b. *Guidelines on the Development of Pre-primary Education*. No. 41. Beijing: State Council. http://www.gov.cn. (国务院。关于当前发展学前教育的若干意见)

———. 2011a. *Development of the Elderly in the 12th Five-Year Plan*. Number 28. Beijing: State Council. http://www.gov.cn/zwgk/2011-09/23. (国务院。中国老龄事业发展"十二五"规划)

———. 2011b. *Guidelines on Chinese Women Development (2011–2020)* and *Guidelines on Chinese Children Development (2011–2020)*. No. 24. Beijing: State Council. http://www.gov.cn/2011-08/08. (国务院。中国妇女发展纲要(2011–2020)。中国儿童发展纲要 (2011–2020))

———. 2011c. *Guidelines on Poverty Reduction and Development of Chinese Rural Areas (2011–2020)*. Beijing: State Council http://www.gov.cn/jrzg/2011-12/01. (国务院。中国农村扶贫开发纲要)

———. 2011d. *Plan for Population Development in the 12th Five Year Plan*. Number 39, 2011. Beijing: State Council. http://www.gov.cn/zwgk/2012-04/10. (国务院。国家人口发展十二五规划)

———. 2011e. *State Council Standing Committee Meeting Decision on Increase of Public Investment on the development of preprimary education*. http://www.gov.cn/ldhd/2011-08/31/content_1937355.htm (国务院常务会议，决定增加财政投入支持发展学前教育)

———. 2011f. *Management of Household Registration System. No. 9.* Beijing: State Council. http://www.gov.cn/zwgk/2012-02/23/content_2075082.htm. (国务院。关于积极稳妥推进户籍管理制度改革)

———. 2012. *Deepening the Reform of Health System in the 12th Five Year Plan.* Document No. 11. Beijing: State Council. http://www.gov.cn/zwgk/2012-03/21/content_2096671.htm (国务院。十二五"期间深化医药卫生体制改革规划暨实施方案)

Vegas, E., and L. Santibañez. 2010. *The Promise of Early Childhood Development in Latin America and the Caribbean.* Washington, DC: World Bank.

World Bank. 2009a. "China Rural Compulsory Education Finance Reform: A Case Study of Gansu." Draft. East Asia Human Development Department. World Bank, Washington, DC.

———. 2009b. "China Education Sector Review: Inputs and Suggestions to China's National Plan for Medium- and Long-Term Educational Reform and Development." Draft. East Asia Human Development Department. World Bank, Washington, DC.

———. 2010a. "World Bank's Inputs to China's 12th Five Year Plan." Draft. China Country Management Unit. World Bank, Washington, DC.

———. 2010b. "Basic Education in Western Areas Project: Implementation Completion Report." Report ICR00001404, World Bank, Washington, DC.

Young, M. E. 1995. "Investing in Young Children." World Bank Discussion Paper 275, World Bank, Washington, DC.

Regressions Results of Multivariate Analysis of the Household Survey on Child Development in Hunan, 2010

Table A.1 Final Results of Multivariate Analysis of the Household Survey on Child Development in Hunan Province, 2010

Variable	(1) Weight	(2) Height	(3) Social development	(4) Cognitive development	(5) Weight	(6) Height	(7) Social development	(8) Cognitive development
Age (months)	0.009	-0.010	-0.001	0.001	0.005	-0.028	-0.001	0.000
	(0.015)	(0.031)	(0.002)	(0.001)	(0.016)	(0.031)	(0.002)	(0.001)
Weight at birth (kg)	0.457	0.964	0.023	0.000	0.435	0.865	0.020	-0.004
	(0.105)***	(0.216)***	(0.015)	(0.008)	(0.108)***	(0.214)***	(0.015)	(0.007)
Female = 1	-0.437	-1.229	-0.010	0.032	-0.433	-1.321	-0.016	0.038
	(0.197)**	(0.405)***	(0.028)	(0.014)**	(0.203)**	(0.404)***	(0.029)	(0.013)***
Family size	-0.018	-0.165	-0.024	-0.002	-0.022	-0.136	-0.032	-0.006
	(0.080)	(0.164)	(0.011)**	(0.006)	(0.081)	(0.161)	(0.012)***	(0.005)
Not raised by parents = 1	0.175	0.572	-0.062	-0.012	0.180	0.536	-0.055	0.005
	(0.305)	(0.626)	(0.043)	(0.022)	(0.323)	(0.641)	(0.046)	(0.021)
Household income (RMB) 2,000–6,000 = 1	0.175	1.113	0.036	0.105	0.093	1.071	-0.001	0.075
	(0.605)	(1.244)	(0.086)	(0.044)**	(0.621)	(1.232)	(0.087)	(0.040)*
Household income (RMB) 6,000–10,000 = 1	0.095	1.152	0.062	0.064	0.096	1.342	0.039	0.033
	(0.566)	(1.164)	(0.081)	(0.041)	(0.581)	(1.152)	(0.082)	(0.038)
Household income (RMB) 10,000–15,000 = 1	0.627	1.510	0.111	0.064	0.501	1.230	0.070	0.030
	(0.563)	(1.157)	(0.080)	(0.041)	(0.582)	(1.155)	(0.082)	(0.038)
Household income (RMB) 15,000–20,000 = 1	0.847	0.997	0.071	0.140	0.704	0.814	0.008	0.094
	(0.571)	(1.173)	(0.081)	(0.041)***	(0.592)	(1.174)	(0.083)	(0.038)**
Household income (RMB) 20,000 or above = 1	0.451	1.473	0.137	0.101	0.378	1.211	0.074	0.042
	(0.563)	(1.158)	(0.080)*	(0.041)**	(0.585)	(1.160)	(0.082)	(0.038)
Rural region = 1	0.880	1.106	0.047	0.047	0.900	0.852	0.066	0.030
	(0.687)	(1.412)	(0.098)	(0.050)	(0.701)	(1.390)	(0.099)	(0.046)
Minority = 1	0.517	2.388	0.022	0.014	0.523	2.651	-0.026	-0.044
	(0.520)	(1.068)**	(0.074)	(0.038)	(0.561)	(1.112)**	(0.079)	(0.037)

(continued next page)

	(1)	(2)	(3)	(4)	(5)	(6)	(7)	(8)
Mother's education = primary	0.636 (0.870)	-2.366 (1.788)	-0.125 (0.124)	0.011 (0.063)	0.616 (0.884)	-2.407 (1.753)	-0.121 (0.126)	-0.011 (0.058)
Mother's education = junior-secondary	0.621 (0.844)	-2.081 (1.734)	-0.139 (0.120)	0.044 (0.061)	0.670 (0.860)	-2.100 (1.707)	-0.146 (0.123)	0.018 (0.057)
Mother's education = senior-secondary	0.963 (0.904)	-1.712 (1.858)	-0.138 (0.129)	0.093 (0.065)	0.900 (0.922)	-1.934 (1.830)	-0.170 (0.131)	0.052 (0.061)
Mother's education = three-year college	0.854 (1.035)	-1.172 (2.128)	0.033 (0.148)	0.174 (0.075)**	0.393 (1.078)	-2.350 (2.138)	-0.023 (0.153)	0.091 (0.071)
Mother's education = university or above	1.820 (1.194)	-0.720 (2.453)	-0.051 (0.170)	0.138 (0.086)	1.560 (1.238)	-1.291 (2.456)	-0.145 (0.176)	0.059 (0.082)
Caregiver's education = primary	0.396 (0.420)	1.266 (0.863)	-0.045 (0.060)	0.066 (0.030)**	0.427 (0.437)	1.345 (0.866)	-0.051 (0.062)	0.039 (0.029)
Caregiver's education = junior-secondary	0.436 (0.463)*	1.726 (0.952)*	-0.082 (0.066)	0.104 (0.034)***	0.549 (0.481)	1.793 (0.954)*	-0.108 (0.069)	0.050 (0.032)
Caregiver's education = senior-secondary	0.387 (0.572)	1.497 (1.176)	-0.099 (0.082)	0.096 (0.041)**	0.524 (0.593)	1.938 (1.176)*	-0.108 (0.085)	0.039 (0.039)
Caregiver's education = three-year college	0.715 (0.822)	2.579 (1.690)	-0.179 (0.117)	0.090 (0.060)	1.264 (0.858)	3.032 (1.701)*	-0.190 (0.122)	0.066 (0.057)
Caregiver's education = university or above	0.648 (0.977)	3.067 (2.007)	-0.049 (0.139)	0.126 (0.071)*	0.872 (1.026)	3.165 (2.036)	0.017 (0.146)	0.114 (0.068)*
Attend kindergarten = 1					0.682 (0.273)**	1.440 (0.541)***	0.093 (0.039)**	0.127 (0.018)***
Attend parent–child class = 1					0.208 (0.322)	-0.568 (0.639)	-0.051 (0.046)	0.050 (0.021)**
Obtain knowledge of early childhood education from TV = 1					-0.206 (0.247)	0.396 (0.490)	-0.013 (0.035)	0.031 (0.016)*

Table A.1 (continued)

Variable	(1) Weight	(2) Height	(3) Social development	(4) Cognitive development	(5) Weight	(6) Height	(7) Social development	(8) Cognitive development
Eat meat or eggs every day = 1					0.714 (0.413)*	0.336 (0.820)		
Eat meat or eggs every 2–3 days = 1					0.413 (0.418)	-0.562 (0.830)		
Eat meat or eggs occasionally = 1					-0.235 (0.459)	-0.265 (0.911)		
Drink milk every day = 1					0.047 (0.371)	1.094 (0.736)		
Drink milk every 2–3 days = 1					-0.151 (0.401)	-0.168 (0.795)		
Drink milk once a week = 1					0.397 (0.590)	2.287 (1.170)*		
Drink milk rarely = 1					-0.438 (0.347)	0.358 (0.687)		
Add calcium = 1					0.053 (0.270)	-0.489 (0.535)		
Unsure about adding calcium = 1					0.410 (0.673)	1.574 (1.334)		
Watch TV less than 1 hour per day = 1					0.699 (0.578)	2.193 (1.147)*	0.179 (0.082)**	0.131 (0.038)***
Watch TV 1–2 hours per day = 1					0.815 (0.598)	3.007 (1.186)**	0.178 (0.085)**	0.141 (0.039)***

Watch TV more than 2 hours per day = 1	0.964 (0.639)	3.416 (1.267)***	0.151 (0.091)*	0.167 (0.042)***
Medical checkup every year = 1	0.036 (0.356)	0.697 (0.706)	0.086 (0.050)*	0.064 (0.023)***
Medical checkup not every year = 1	0.271 (0.309)	0.312 (0.612)	0.063 (0.044)	0.022 (0.020)
Unsure about medical checkup = 1	0.532 (0.628)	-1.940 (1.246)	0.017 (0.086)	0.003 (0.040)
Eat fruit every day = 1	-0.184 (0.415)	-0.833 (0.824)		
Eat fruit every 2-3 days = 1	0.213 (0.439)	-1.062 (0.870)		
Eat fruit occasionally = 1	0.493 (0.429)	0.107 (0.850)		
Immunization whether free or not = 1	-1.363 (0.847)	-2.221 (1.679)	-0.072 (0.120)	0.079 (0.055)
Immunization only when free = 1	-1.172 (0.875)	-2.614 (1.735)	-0.134 (0.124)	0.069 (0.057)
Unsure about immunization = 1	0.667 (1.131)	-1.648 (2.242)	-0.192 (0.161)	0.081 (0.074)
Read to children 1-2 times per week = 1			-0.058 (0.046)	0.051 (0.021)**
Read to children more than 2 times per week = 1			0.002 (0.051)	0.125 (0.024)***
Play with children less than 1 hour per day = 1			0.067 (0.035)*	0.013 (0.016)

(continued next page)

143

Table A.1 (continued)

Variable	(1) Weight	(2) Height	(3) Social development	(4) Cognitive development	(5) Weight	(6) Height	(7) Social development	(8) Cognitive development
Play with children 1–2 hours per day = 1							0.081 (0.057)	0.000 (0.026)
Play with children more than 2 hours per day = 1							0.099 (0.080)	-0.042 (0.037)
Sometimes punish = 1							0.093 (0.058)	-0.025 (0.027)
Never punish = 1							0.082 (0.072)	-0.039 (0.033)
Don't care about punishment = 1							-0.003 (0.216)	0.034 (0.100)
Constant	13.173 (3.114)***	90.731 (6.400)***	2.924 (0.444)***	0.098 (0.225)	9.642 (3.279)***	97.321 (6.503)***	3.558 (0.467)***	0.533 (0.216)**
Number of observations	803	803	803	803	786	786	786	786
R-squared	0.33	0.35	0.21	0.44	0.37	0.40	0.25	0.56
Adjusted R-squared	0.25	0.27	0.11	0.37	0.26	0.30	0.12	0.49

Source: Authors.

Note: Standard errors in parentheses. * significant at 10%; ** significant at 5%; *** significant at 1%.

www.ingramcontent.com/pod-product-compliance
ightning Source LLC
nbersburg PA
961739270326
CB00011B/2305